AF496543

FRANCIS FRITH'S

ELY & THE FENS

PHOTOGRAPHIC MEMORIES

FRANK MEERES is senior archivist at the Norfolk Record Office with special responsibility for the records of Norwich Cathedral. He has written many books on the history of East Anglia, including *A History of Bury St Edmunds, Not of this World - the Monastic Houses of Norfolk,* and *A History of Norwich.* In the year 2000 he and fellow historian Michael Boon published an illustrated history of Great Yarmouth which was given to every child in the town in celebration of the new millennium. He has given many talks and classes on all aspects of local and family history.

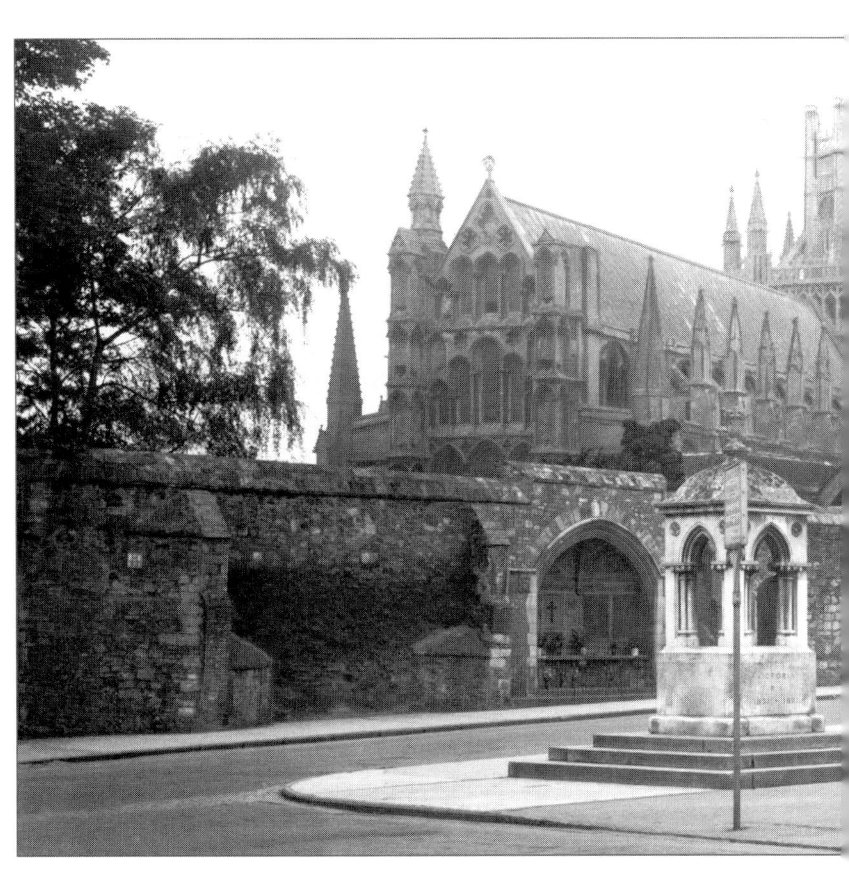

FRANCIS FRITH'S
PHOTOGRAPHIC MEMORIES

ELY & THE FENS

PHOTOGRAPHIC MEMORIES

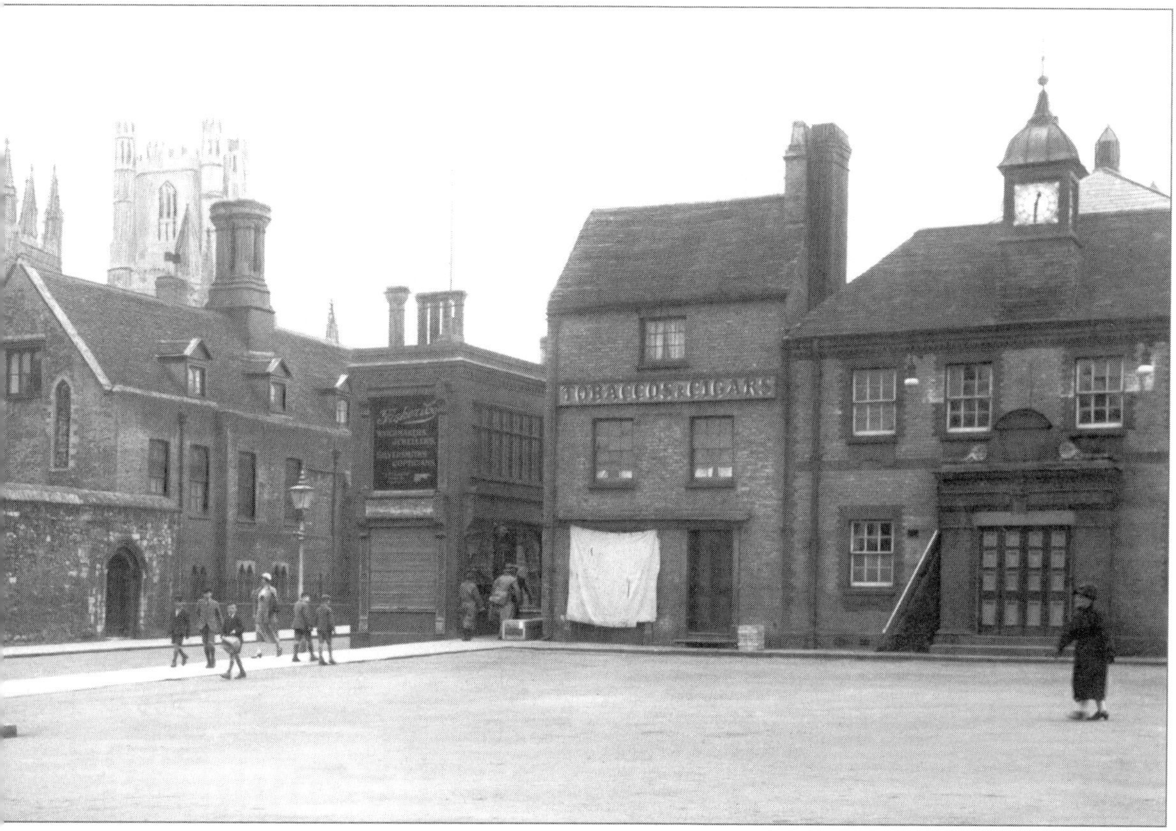

FRANK MEERES

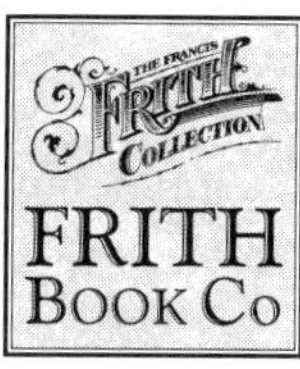

First published in the United Kingdom in 2003 by
Frith Book Company Ltd

Paperback Edition 2003
ISBN 1-85937-615-0

British Library Cataloguing in Publication Data

Francis Frith's Ely & The Fens
Frank Meeres

Frith Book Company Ltd
Frith's Barn, Teffont,
Salisbury, Wiltshire SP3 5QP
Tel: +44 (0) 1722 716 376
Email: info@francisfrith.co.uk
www.francisfrith.co.uk

Printed and bound in Great Britain

Front Cover: **KING'S LYNN,** *Southgate 1891* 28760

Frontispiece: **ELY,** *Market Place 1925* 78276

AS WITH ANY HISTORICAL DATABASE THE FRITH ARCHIVE IS CONSTANTLY
BEING CORRECTED AND IMPROVED AND THE PUBLISHERS WOULD
WELCOME INFORMATION ON OMISSIONS OR INACCURACIES

CONTENTS

FRANCIS FRITH
VICTORIAN PIONEER

FRANCIS FRITH, founder of the world-famous photographic archive, was a complex and multi-talented man. A devout Quaker and a highly successful Victorian businessman, he was philosophic by nature and pioneering in outlook.

By 1855 he had already established a wholesale grocery business in Liverpool, and sold it for the astonishing sum of £200,000, which is the equivalent today of over £15,000,000. Now a multi-millionaire, he was able to indulge his passion for travel. As a child he had pored over travel books written by early explorers, and his fancy and imagination had been stirred by family holidays to the sublime mountain regions of Wales and Scotland. 'What a land of spirit-stirring and enriching scenes and places!' he had written. He was to return to these scenes of grandeur in later years to 'recapture the thousands of vivid and tender memories', but with a different purpose. Now in his thirties, and captivated by the new science of photography, Frith set out on a series of pioneering journeys up the Nile and to the Near East that occupied him from 1856 until 1860.

INTRIGUE AND EXPLORATION

These far-flung journeys were packed with intrigue and adventure. In his life story, written when he was sixty-three, Frith tells of being held captive by bandits, and of fighting 'an awful midnight battle to the very point of surrender with a deadly pack of hungry, wild dogs'. Wearing flowing Arab costume, Frith arrived at Akaba by camel seventy years before Lawrence of Arabia, where he encountered 'desert princes and rival sheikhs, blazing with jewel-hilted swords'.

He was the first photographer to venture beyond the sixth cataract of the Nile. Africa was still the mysterious 'Dark Continent', and Stanley and Livingstone's historic meeting was a decade into the future. The conditions for picture taking confound belief. He laboured for hours in his wicker dark-room in the sweltering heat of the desert, while the volatile chemicals fizzed dangerously in their trays. Back in London he exhibited his photographs and was 'rapturously cheered' by members of the Royal Society. His reputation as a photographer was made overnight.

VENTURE OF A LIFE-TIME

Characteristically, Frith quickly spotted the opportunity to create a new business as a specialist publisher of photographs. He lived in an era of immense and sometimes violent change.

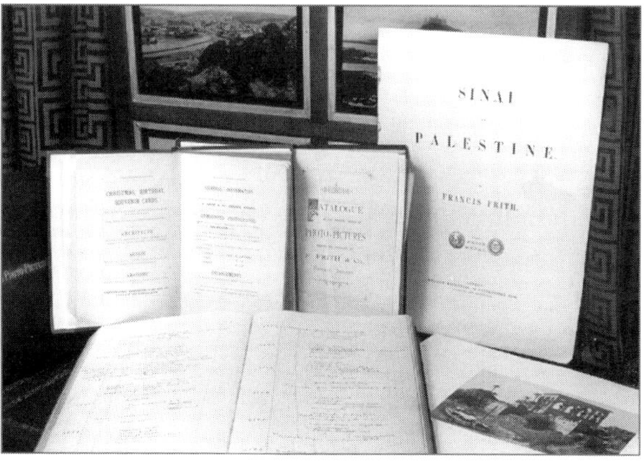

For the poor in the early part of Victoria's reign work was exhausting and the hours long, and people had precious little free time to enjoy themselves. Most had no transport other than a cart or gig at their disposal, and rarely travelled far beyond the boundaries of their own town or village. However, by the 1870s the railways had threaded their way across the country, and Bank Holidays and half-day Saturdays had been made obligatory by Act of Parliament. All of a sudden the working man and his family were able to enjoy days out and see a little more of the world.

With typical business acumen, Francis Frith foresaw that these new tourists would enjoy having souvenirs to commemorate their days out. In 1860 he married Mary Ann Rosling and set out on a new career: his aim was to photograph every city, town and village in Britain. For the next thirty years he travelled the country by train and by pony and trap, producing fine photographs of seaside resorts and beauty spots that were keenly bought by millions of Victorians. These prints were painstakingly pasted into family albums and pored over during the dark nights of winter, rekindling precious memories of summer excursions.

THE RISE OF FRITH & CO

Frith's studio was soon supplying retail shops all over the country. To meet the demand he gath-

ered about him a small team of photographers, and published the work of independent artist-photographers of the calibre of Roger Fenton and Francis Bedford. In order to gain some understanding of the scale of Frith's business one only has to look at the catalogue issued by Frith & Co in 1886: it runs to some 670 pages, listing not only many thousands of views of the British Isles but also many photographs of most European countries, and China, Japan, the USA and Canada - note the sample page shown here from the hand-written Frith & Co ledgers recording the pictures. By 1890 Frith had created the greatest specialist photographic publishing company in the world, with over 2,000 sales outlets - more than the combined number that Boots and WH Smith have today! The picture on the nest page shows the Frith & Co display board at Ingleton in the Yorkshire Dales. Beautifully constructed with mahogany frame and gilt inserts, it could display up to a dozen local scenes.

POSTCARD BONANZA

The ever-popular holiday postcard we know today took many years to develop. In 1870 the Post Office issued the first plain cards, with a pre-printed stamp on one face. In 1894 they allowed other publishers' cards to be sent through the mail with an attached adhesive half-penny stamp. Demand grew rapidly, and in 1895 a new size of postcard was permitted called the court card, but there was little room for illustration. In 1899, a year after Frith's death, a new card measuring 5.5 x 3.5 inches became the standard format, but it was not until 1902 that the divided back came into being, so that the address and message could be on one face and a full-size illustration on the other. Frith & Co were in the vanguard of postcard development: Frith's sons Eustace and Cyril continued their father's monumental task, expanding the number of views offered to the public and recording more

5	Queens College, View from the Garden		
6	St Catherine's College	+	
7	Senate House & Library	+	+
8			
9	Gerrard Hostel Bridge	+	+ +
30	Geological Museum		
1	Addenbrooke's Hospital	+	
2	St Mary's Church	+	
3	Fitzwilliam Museum, Pitt Press &c	+	
4		+	
5	Buxton, The Crescent	+	
6	" The Colonnade	+	
7	" Public Gardens	+	
8	"	+	
9	Haddon Hall, View from the Terrace	+	
40	Miller's Dale	+	

and more places in Britain, as the coasts and countryside were opened up to mass travel.

Francis Frith had died in 1898 at his villa in Cannes, his great project still growing. The archive he created continued in business for another seventy years. By 1970 it contained over a third of a million pictures showing 7,000 British towns and villages.

FRANCIS FRITH'S LEGACY

Frith's legacy to us today is of immense significance and value, for the magnificent archive of evocative photographs he created provides a unique record of change in the cities, towns and villages throughout Britain over a century and more. Frith and his fellow studio photographers revisited locations many times down the years to update their views, compiling for us an enthralling and colourful pageant of British life and character.

We are fortunate that Frith was dedicated to recording the minutiae of everyday life. For it is this sheer wealth of visual data, the painstaking chronicle of changes in dress, transport, street layouts, buildings, housing, engineering and landscape that captivates us so much today. His remarkable images offer us a powerful link with the past and with the lives of our ancestors.

THE VALUE OF THE ARCHIVE TODAY

Computers have now made it possible for Frith's many thousands of images to be accessed almost instantly. Frith's images are increasingly used as visual resources, by social historians, by researchers into genealogy and ancestry, by architects and town planners, and by teachers involved in local history projects.

In addition, the archive offers every one of us an opportunity to examine the places where we and our families have lived and worked down the years. Highly successful in Frith's own era, the archive is now, a century and more on, entering a new phase of popularity. Historians consider the Francis Frith Collection to be of prime national importance. It is the only archive of its kind remaining in private ownership. Francis Frith's archive is now housed in an historic timber barn in the beautiful village of Teffont in Wiltshire. Its founder would not recognize the archive office as it is today. In place of the many thousands of dusty boxes containing glass plate negatives and an all-pervading odour of photographic chemicals, there are now ranks of computer screens. He would be amazed to watch his images travelling round the world at unimaginable speeds through internet lines.

The archive's future is both bright and exciting. Francis Frith, with his unshakeable belief in making photographs available to the greatest number of people, would undoubtedly approve of what is being done today with his lifetime's work. His photographs depicting our shared past are now bringing pleasure and enlightenment to millions around the world a century and more after his death.

ELY & THE FENS
AN INTRODUCTION

'Above us only sky', wrote John Lennon in his song 'Imagine', and it is the sky in all its moods that dominates the Fens. Many of the photographs in this book capture the sense of a view of a vast, often treeless distance, with only the works of man – windmills and church spires - standing out against the horizon.

Historically, the Fens extended into five counties – Cambridgeshire, Norfolk, Suffolk, Lincolnshire and into the county of Huntingdonshire, which was abolished under Local Government reforms in 1974. The geology is simple: the Fens are an area of flat sedimentary deposits or huge flood plain between two ridges of higher land. The soil of the northern fens is mainly of marine deposits, while that of the southern fens is peat deposited by the rivers of the East Midlands meeting the seas of the Wash. Farming over the centuries has eroded much of the peat, so that great areas of the southern fens are now in fact below sea level.

Sea levels are currently rising, and it is disputed to what extent global warming is causing this. However, sea levels have been falling and rising throughout the ages. In medieval times the coastline of the Wash was 12 miles further inland

ELY, *The view from the West Tower c1955* E34068

than it is today, and the southern fens were marshland. Settlement was only possible on islands rising out of this marsh. Place-names that end in '-ey' or '-ea', such as Manea, Thorney and Ramsey, preserve this history: 'eye' is the Old English word for an island.

The entire history of man in the Fens has been the struggle with excess water, both coming in from the sea and flooding from the rivers. The whole area is, in fact, a man-made landscape. The Romans began this work 2,000 years ago, building the Car Dyke and other channels, probably including the Old Lode at Burwell.

Although the work stopped for several centuries, the Saxons eventually picked it up again. Monasteries were established on the islands and began the work of draining surrounding areas. This came to a sudden halt in most places when marauding Danes pillaged and burnt the monastic houses in the 9th century—Thorney Abbey preserves a powerful relic of this time in the skull of Abbot Theodore, who was killed while praying at his high altar.

However, the rule of the Danes was short-lived. The Saxons came back and brought a new type of monastic house, inhabited by black-robed monks following the Rule established by Saint Benedict. From these settlements the work of drainage began again. Local villagers also worked to control the sea, often working in co-operation with neighbouring communities. There is an almost continuous sea wall, now several miles inland, running along the former southern limit of the Wash. The historian William Dugdale called it the Roman Bank, and the name is still in use: this is unfortunate, as it was not made by the Romans, but rather several hundred years later.

The great age of drainage was the 17th century, when the Bedford Levels were drained under the direction of the Dutch engineer Cornelius Vermuyden. It was he who built the two Bedford rivers running straight as arrows through the heart of Fenland, with the Denver sluice controlling both the downward flow of fresh water and the upward flow of the tides. The process has continued, with other sluices and channels made in the succeeding centuries, some of which are shown in this book. In the 1960s the work was 'completed': excess water from the Fens is now tunnelled all the way to Essex to serve the needs of the Home Counties. For now, man seems to be in control, but it is impossible to be sure how long this will last: one of the most devastating floods in the history of Fenland occurred as recently as 1947.

Not everyone liked the new landscape. Although it meant wealth for the big landowners with their new fields full of cattle or of corn, for the poor man it meant a loss of cheap food in the form of fish, eels and wildfowl, and also a loss of fuel and reeds from the marshes. Many times in the 17th century villagers tried to destroy sluices and drainage banks. As it was not legal for people to gather together without a specific purpose, they sometimes pretended to be meeting for a game of football – an association between football and crowd violence that continues into the present century!

Despite the shortage of building stone, the area is one dominated by church spires. A feature almost unique to the Fens is that of the eight-sided tower, or octagon. The most dramatic is at Ely, but other examples include the spectacular Boston Stump. Although the Fens were once drained by windmills, these have all disappeared, to be replaced by more powerful steam engines, and later by electric pumps. However, several corn windmills do survive.

Naturally, Fenland has always been an area where water traffic has dominated, with major ports at Boston and Lynn, and smaller boats conveying goods up the Nene, Ouse and Welland rivers. As this traffic has largely died out in the 20th century, it has been replaced by the leisure use of the same waters.

'Fen Tigers' have always been known as independent-minded, tough characters. They do not always have a good image to the outsider, who talks of webbed feet and of men on stilts. (The latter claim has been true for many hundreds of years: in the 14th century it is recorded that a boy who was drowned collecting ducks' eggs in the marshes wore 'feet of wood'. These were surely stilts rather than mere clogs, which would not be thought worth a mention). The contribution of men of the Fens to the volunteer effort in the First World War has not been well enough recorded. Many did not come back, and the numerous war memorials in these photographs remind us of their sacrifice. Many of these memorials now include additional names from the Second World War.

These photographs capture the natural and man-made features of Fenland in the late 19th and the 20th centuries, but many evoke an almost timeless landscape that has enchanted people for centuries and will surely continue to enchant the generations to come.

DOWNHAM MARKET, *The Bridge c1965* D149034

ELY, THE QUEEN OF THE FENS

ELY CATHEDRAL, which can be seen from up to twenty miles away on a clear day, is one of the most stirring sights in Fenland. Etheldreda founded a religious community for women here in 673: she died just six years later. Like so many of the Fenland monasteries, it was destroyed by marauding Danes in 870. It was re-founded as a male religious house following the rule of St Benedict. Tradition says that some of the monks were unwilling to embrace the newly imposed rule of celibacy; they were punished by being turned into eels! Etheldreda herself gave a new word to the language. She was known locally as Audrey, and the cheapness of stuff sold at the annual fair at Ely, known as St Audrey's Fair, gave rise to the word 'tawdry'.

ELY, *The Cathedral c1878* 10953

Here we have the classic view of the west front, lop-sided in appearance since the north-west (left-hand) transept and tower fell down in the late Middle Ages. The cannon in the foreground is a Russian one, captured at Sebastopol in the Crimean War in the 1850s.

ELY, *The Cathedral from the River 1891* 28179

This photograph shows the sharp rise from river level to the cathedral. It is easy to imagine how a local Saxon leader like Hereward the Wake could defend Ely from the invading Norman army. Unfortunately, the monks of the abbey did not wish to be defended: it was they who told the Normans the way to capture Ely!

◀ **ELY**
The Cathedral from the Meadows 1898
40867

This is another classic view of the cathedral, taken from the south; it shows the great length of the building. At 535ft, Ely is the fourth longest cathedral in England. This view also shows clearly the unique eight-sided central tower.

ELY
The Cathedral, the Inner West Porch 1891 28205

Having admired the outside of the cathedral, the visitor enters
through this porch, known as the Galilee Porch. It was begun before
1215, and the ceiling vault dates from about 1250, the earliest major
piece of vaulting in the cathedral.

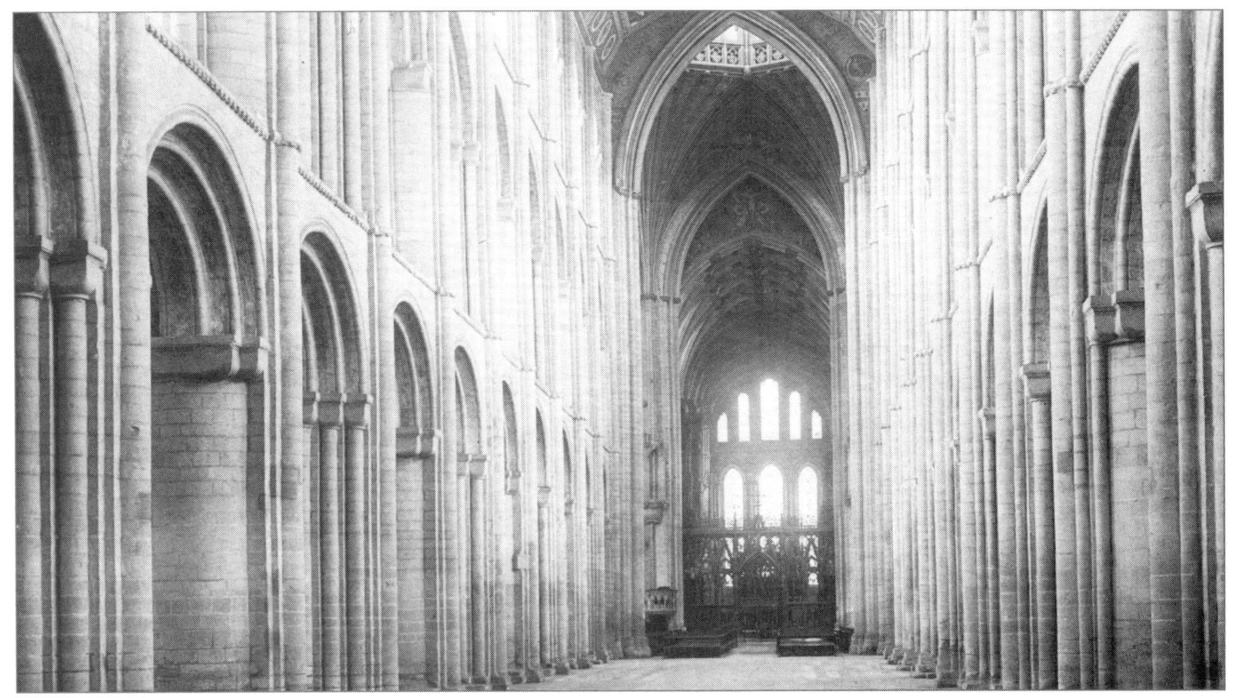

▲ **ELY**
The Cathedral, the Nave looking East 1891 28191

Passing through the porch, the visitor is greeted with this stunning view: three storeys of Norman arches lead the eye to the central space and the choir beyond.

► **ELY**
The Cathedral, the Choir looking West 1891 28194

This is taken from the east end of the cathedral, looking back down the choir and nave. The choir stalls are 14th-century. They all have misericords, wooden brackets on which the monks could lean for support during a long service. They include wonderfully imaginative carvings, such as monkeys, a bear, a man falling from a horse and a woman beating a fox!

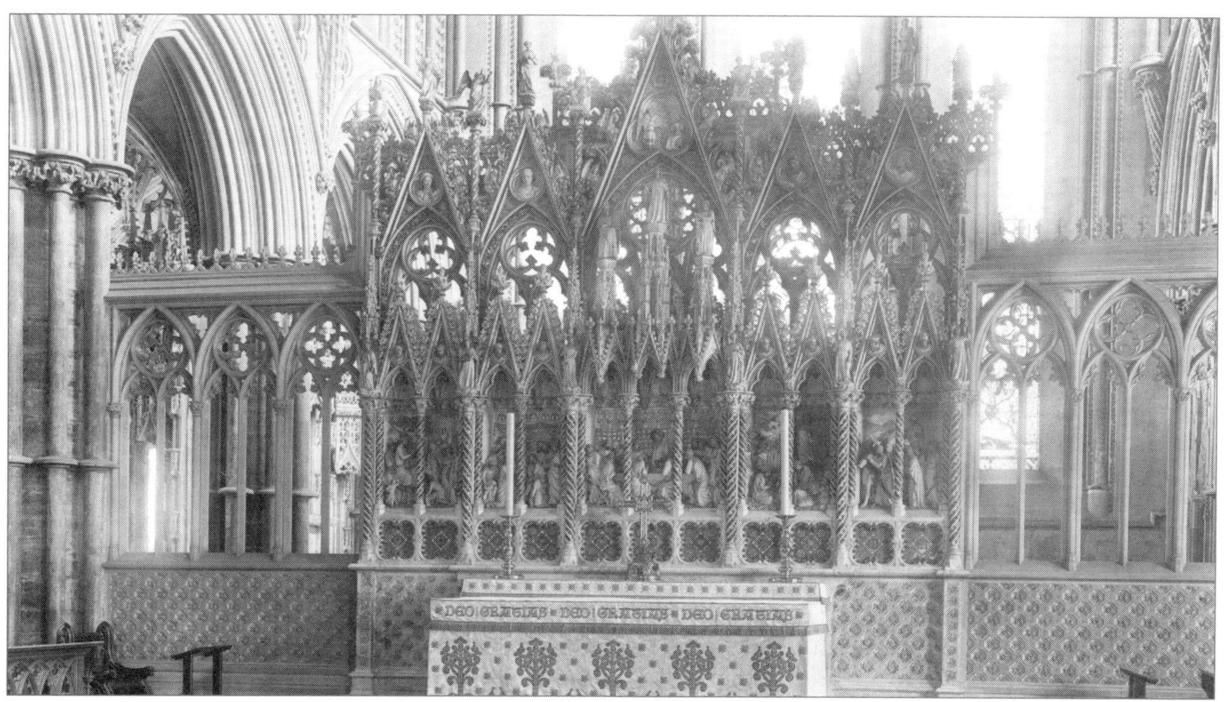

▲ **ELY**
The Cathedral, the Reredos 1898
40872

The high altar is the most sacred part of the church, and its importance is often emphasised by a reredos, or screen, behind and above it. Most were destroyed at the Reformation, and those seen in churches today are usually Victorian. This grand structure is the work of the Victorian architect Gilbert Scott.

◄ **ELY**
The Cathedral, North Choir Aisle 1891 28200

Passages or aisles run to the south and north of the choir. The circular stairway leads up to the organ loft. We can see the organ case clearly in photograph 28194. Both the case and the stairway are again designs by Gilbert Scott.

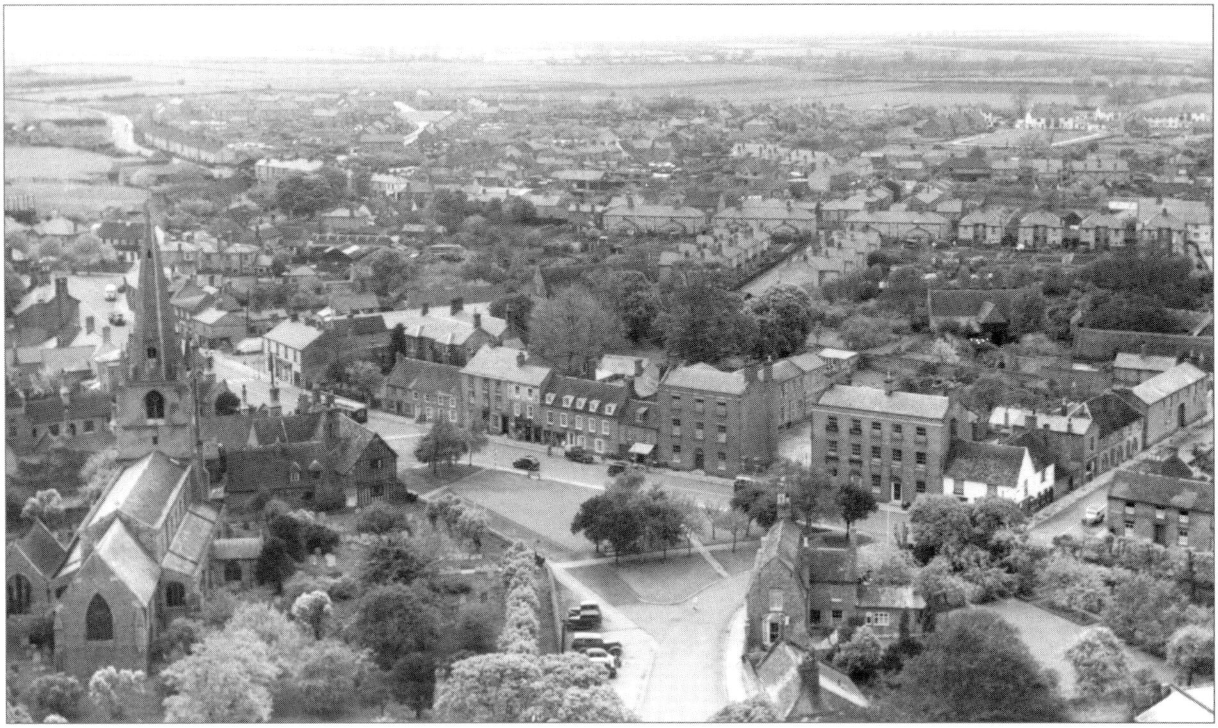

▲ ELY
The View from the West Tower of the Cathedral c1955 E34066

We are looking west. The church (left) is St Mary's. The Littleport rioters (see L366010, page 64) were buried in St Mary's churchyard, and there is a plaque to them on the wall of the tower. Oliver Cromwell lived in the house immediately to the right of the church tower from 1636 to 1647.

◄ ELY
The Cathedral, St Catherine's Chapel 1891 28203

The chapel at the west end of the cathedral has Norman architecture, with zigzag decoration over the archway and intersecting arches along the wall. The font is once more the work of Gilbert Scott; an 18th-century font formerly in Ely Cathedral is now in the church at nearby Prickwillow.

 **ELY**

The View from the West Tower of the Cathedral c1955 E34071

This photograph gives a close view of the wooden octagonal turret rising out of the larger stone octagonal tower. The octagon was built to the design of the cathedral sacrist Adam de Walsingham; it replaced the central tower of the cathedral, which fell down in 1322.

▶ **ELY**

The Cathedral, the Prior's Door 1891 28190

This wonderful doorway dates from about 1140. Above the door is a carving of Christ in majesty, with an angel on each side. The carvings on the door surrounds include designs of people at work and the signs of the zodiac. Like the woodcarvers of the choir stalls, the stonemasons were clearly encouraged to use their imaginations!

ELY
The View from the West Tower of the Cathedral c1955 E34064

We are now looking north east: we can see the Market Place on the extreme right of the photograph, with the Corn Exchange to its left. The chimney in the distance is that of the sugar beet factory at Queen Adelaide, opened in 1925.

ELY
The Cathedral from the Palace Gardens 1898 40870

This is the garden front of the Bishop's Palace, built for Bishop Laney
(1667-1675). To the right is part of the enormous plane tree in the
Bishop's garden: it was planted in the 16th century, and is said to be
the largest plane tree in Britain and possibly in Europe!

ELY

Market Place 1925 78276

The monument (left) celebrates the Diamond Jubilee of Queen Victoria in 1897. Behind it, built into the cathedral wall, is an unusual First World War memorial in the form of a shrine. The building with the clock (right) is the Public Room, with a tobacconist to the left and Fisher's, watchmakers, between it and the cathedral precinct.

► **ELY**
*The Square and
the Cathedral
c1955* E34076

Thirty years after
photograph 78276, the
watchmakers and
tobacconist remain,
but the Victoria
memorial has gone –
it was moved to
Archers Street in 1939.
The Public Room
became a cinema in
1934: the films on
offer at the time of the
photograph are 'Too
Young to Kiss' and
'Mask of the Avenger'.

◄ **ELY**
*The Cathedral, the
West Front c1955*
E34011

Here we have a fine view
of the west tower, with its
octagonal upper section.
Note the gas-lamp
(centre left): it was only
in 1955 that electric
lighting replaced gas in
the streets of the town.
The beautiful half-
timbered house on the
right of the photograph is
St Mary's House; a
plaque on the building
dates it to about 1550.

▲ **ELY,** *Old Houses, Silver Street c1955* E34022

This is the finest row of late medieval houses in Ely. The house on the left is of stone, while the one on the right has the timbered upper storey characteristic of 16th-century houses. The Cambridgeshire Cottage Improvement Society has since beautifully restored these houses; medieval wall paintings were discovered while this work was being carried out.

◄ **ELY**
The Walpole Porta c1955 E34023

Gatehouses are often the most complete surviving buildings of monasteries. Like many such gateways, this has two archways on its outer face, one for pedestrians and one for carts. Inside there is just one large archway. The gate is named 'Walpole' after the prior who had it built in about 1400.

▼ **ELY,** *The Porta and the Cathedral from Barton Square c1955* E34018

The walls to the left of the Porta mark the boundary of the medieval priory. The building on the left, at the corner of Silver Street, is Hereward House. It was built in 1881 as a dormitory for Ely School, and its name is one of the few reminders in the town of its legendary hero Hereward the Wake.

► **ELY**
Fore Hill 1925 78274

The shop on the extreme left is Sturton and Howard, a chemist's, who had already been established on the site for a quarter of a century. The first shop on the other side of the street is A W Morris, gentleman's outfitters. The prominent 'T' sign over the street (centre) belongs to the shop of Joshua Taylor, clothiers.

◄ **ELY**
Fore Hill c1955
E34007

It is thirty years after 78274, and the photograph was taken on a summer day, judging from the awnings and the dresses. The car now predominates, but there are still plenty of bicycles on show. Most of the shops have changed hands since 1925, but Sturton and Howard (left) are still flourishing.

► **ELY**
St Mary's Street
1925 78273

The three-storeyed house with extensions (centre) is Bedford House. It has two fine Georgian doorways, the right-hand one carrying the coat of arms of the Bedford Level Corporation. Its Latin motto can be translated as 'Dryness is Pleasing'. Bedford House became the High School for Girls in 1905.

ELY
*St Peter's Church
1891* 28207

This church was built at the expense of Catherine Sparke as a memorial to her husband Edward, who was a canon at Ely Cathedral. It opened the year before this photograph was taken. In 1893 a rood screen was erected in the church, probably the first of many such works by Ninian Comper.

ELY, *The Theological College c1960* E34061

The college opened in 1881: the architect was J P St Aubyn, who also built St Peter's church (28207). Men would train here for the priesthood, and be ordained in the cathedral just across the green. As the number of people wishing to become clergymen declined, the college became surplus to requirements; Ely School now uses the building.

ELY, *The River Ouse c1955* E34014

The many waterways of the fens are a paradise for rowers - and in winter for skaters. These young oarsmen are from the Cathedral School, but Cambridge University rowers also used the Ouse near Ely to practice for their annual boat race against Oxford.

ELY, *The River Ouse and the Cutter Inn c1955* E34016

Pleasure boats line the far bank of the Ouse - the area was once known as Babylon. The inn-sign of the Cutter shows a ship in full sail at sea; however, the inn is probably named after the cutters, the men who dug the new cut between Ely and Littleport in the 1830s.

ELY

The River c1960 E34059

The Quay Brewery is on the right of the photograph. Beer has been
brewed in Ely for at least 750 years; the monks once complained
that their beer 'was so weak that the pigs would not drink of it'.
In 1960 this brewery was owned by Hall, Cutlack and Harlock, a
combination of local firms.

THE NORFOLK FENS

IT IS THE Fens of western Norfolk, along with the Broads in the east of the county, which have given the county its reputation for being flat. Other parts of the county actually have some quite respectable slopes, including those rising to the ridge along west Norfolk that marks the eastern edge of Fenland.

The area is dominated by Lynn, King's Lynn since the 16th century, but in the Middle Ages Bishop's Lynn and one of the busiest ports in England. The Norfolk Fens also include the Denver Sluice, the most important monument in Fenland to man's attempts to control nature here.

KING'S LYNN, *The Quay 1898* 40893

Here we see two sailing ships and a paddle steamer on the mudflats of the river Great Ouse at low tide. Loading and unloading here has always been tricky because of the tidal range. Because of this, two docks were built to the seaward side of the quay, 600 yards beyond the building at the far end of the quay in this photograph.

KING'S LYNN
The Customs House 1898 40878

The Customs House was built in 1683 by a local gentleman-
architect, Henry Bell. It was built as a Merchants' Exchange, but it
was bought by the Collector of Customs in 1718 (the Customs were
already leasing part of the building). This is the Purfleet Quay: the
quay we can see in 40893 is off to the right of the photograph.

KING'S LYNN
Southgate 1891 28760

Towns, like monasteries, needed defences against their enemies.
Most town gates were pulled down in the 18th century because they
blocked the roads: this is a rare survival. The stone face of the gate is
the south side, which visitors to the town would see first.

KING'S LYNN
Norfolk Street 1891
28769

The large building to the centre right of the picture is Fiddaman's Hotel. On the far right is Plowright and Pratt, ironmongers. The boy and his dog stand below an advertisement for the 'Zoedone and Herb Beer' factory, a business carried out in the yard behind the ironmongers.

KING'S LYNN
High Street 1891
28770

The nearest shops on both sides of the road are tailors; the one on the right offers suits to measure at prices from 30 shillings to 84 shillings, accompanied by the stern warning 'Cash Only'. In the centre of the street a horse has left evidence of its recent passage.

▲ **KING'S LYNN,** *High Street c1955* K28035

Half a century has passed since 28770 was taken; the horse has given way to a variety of transport types - cars, seemingly careless of 'Keep Left' regulations, mix with bicycles, while the window-cleaner pushes his cart. Purfleet Road to the left leads down to the Customs House shown in 40878 (page 32).

◀ **KING'S LYNN**
*Tuesday Market Place
1898* 40886

Lynn has two market places, each used on just the one day in the week, as their names indicate. This explains the temporary-looking nature of the stalls and tables from which items are being sold. The stone-fronted building at the back is the Corn Exchange, built in 1854.

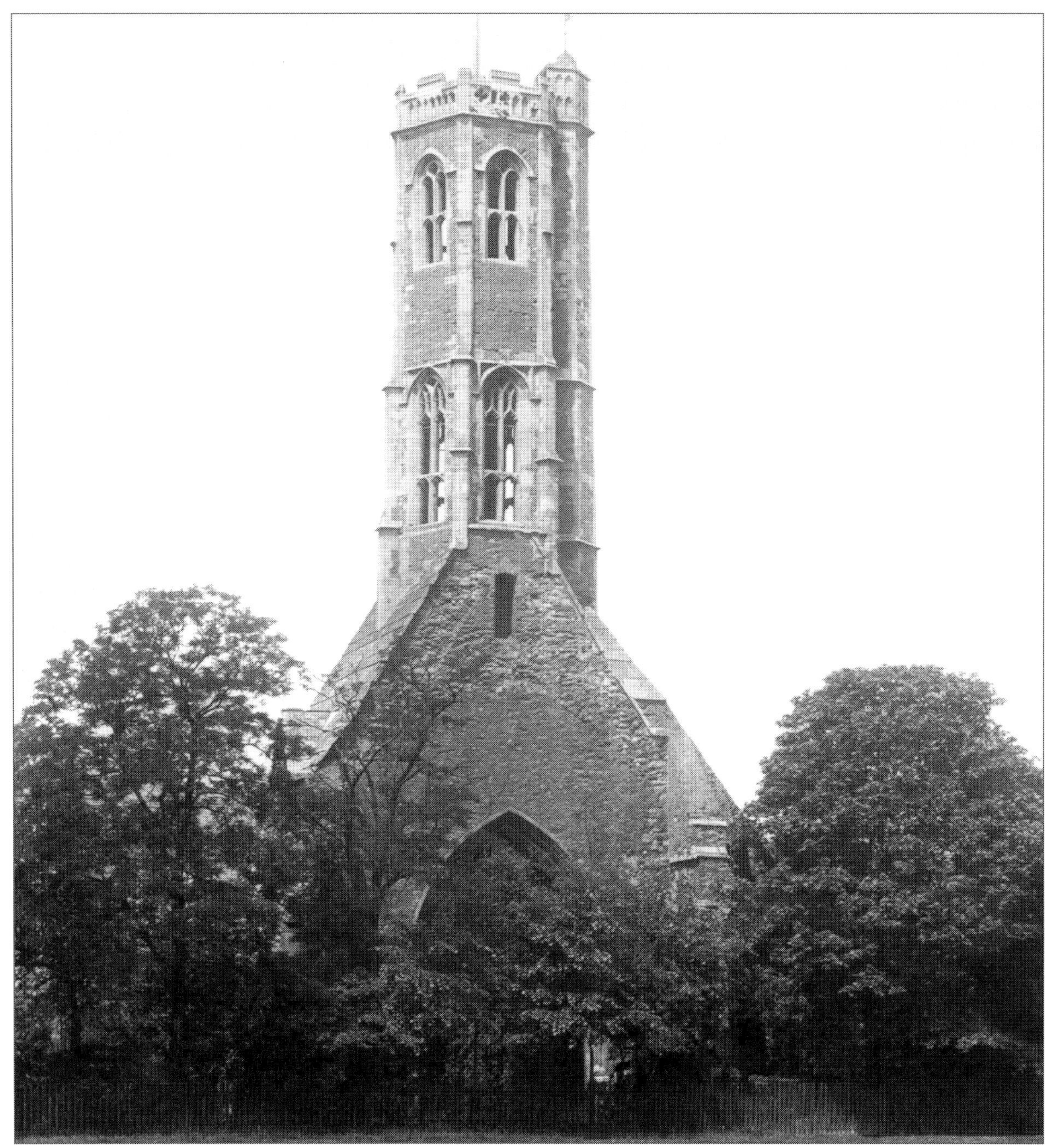

KING'S LYNN, *Grey Friars Tower 1891* 28768

The grey friars were Franciscans, followers of St Francis of Assisi. One famous friar here in the 14th century was Nicholas of Lynn, astronomer and explorer. He used the top of this tower as his observatory and also made several voyages into the Atlantic Ocean - he may even have reached America 130 years before Christopher Columbus.

KING'S LYNN
Red Mount Chapel 1898 40890

This unique building stands in an area of public space known as
The Walks. The first Walk was laid out as a public promenade as
early as 1713. The area was extended several times over the next 180
years, a beautiful legacy to generations of Lynn residents. The chapel
was built in 1485 to serve pilgrims passing through Lynn on their
way to the shrine at Walsingham.

KING'S LYNN
The Town Hall 1891
28754

Elderly inhabitants of the town sit in front of the Guildhall, with its flushwork pattern of flint and limestone and church-like window. It was built in the 1420s, with the building to the left being added two centuries later. Note the sundial on the pediment of the 18th-century building to the right, which was built as the borough gaol.

KING'S LYNN
St Margaret's Church 1891 28761

The 'twin' west towers are in fact very different in style: the left-hand
tower is mainly Norman, while the right-hand tower is 15th-century.
Both of the churches in Lynn had spires that blew down in a tremendous
gale in 1741; many ships were also lost in the storm. This church
contains two wonderful 14th-century brasses, one of which includes an
image of a windmill. Tradition says that there was once a third equally
magnificent brass, but that it was sold for ten shillings!

KING'S LYNN, *St Nicholas's Church, the South Porch 1891* 28766

This porch dates from the early 15th century, and has very rich carvings; it must have looked
stunning when its niches were filled with statues of saints. The lion and eagle statues on the
pinnacles have disappeared since this photograph was taken.

GAYWOOD
The Clock Tower c1965 G189020

The clock tower was built as a memorial to the men of Gaywood killed in the First World War, one of the many imaginative memorials in Fenland. The names of those who died in the Second World War were added, but later the tower was thought to be an obstruction to traffic and it was dismantled. After protests from locals it was eventually re-erected, but in a less prominent position.

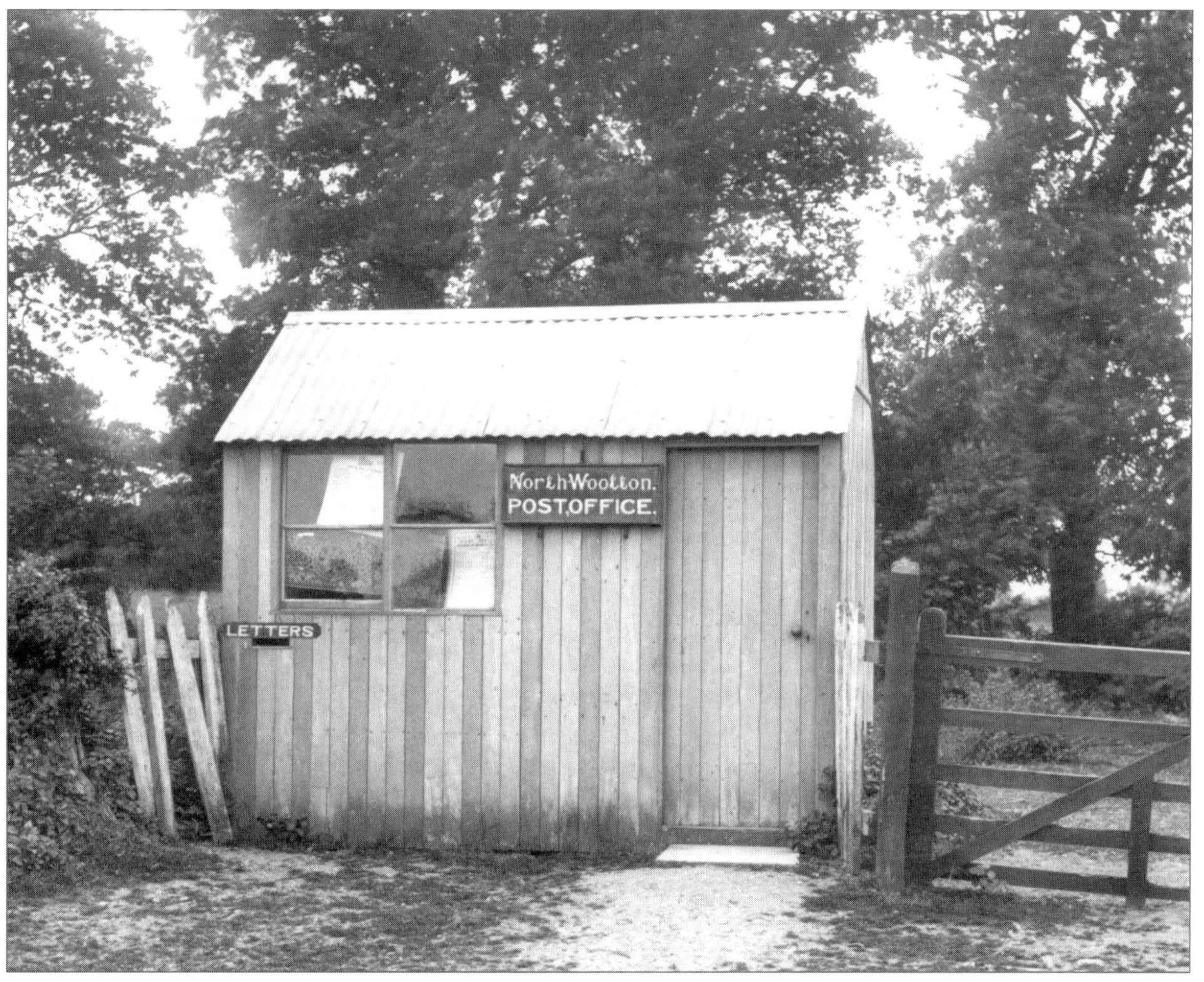

NORTH WOOTTON
The Post Office 1908 60035

The village of North Wootton had a population of under 300 people at the
time of this photograph; even so, it is hard to believe that this isolated
shed can have been its post office on more than a very temporary basis.
The sub-postmistress in 1908 was Mrs Paine. Letters were received from
King's Lynn twice a day, and dispatched once.

HILGAY
*The Bridge and
Bridge House c1955*
H308001

The pleasure cruiser has
replaced goods traffic on
the River Ouse. However,
folk memories live long
in the Fens. The writer
William Dutt records
that he talked to a boy
on this bridge in 1904
who told him that King
Charles hid nearby. This
would have been in
1646, when he escaped
from Oxford and made
his way north to
surrender to the Scots.

CLENCHWARTON, *The School c1965* C416015

Sherlock Holmes called Board Schools 'beacons of light'. Established under the Education Act of 1870, they aimed to build
schools in places where religious groups had not already done so, thus providing elementary education to every child in the
country for the first time. They have their own style of architecture, and often, as here, they are almost two schools put
together, one for girls and one for boys.

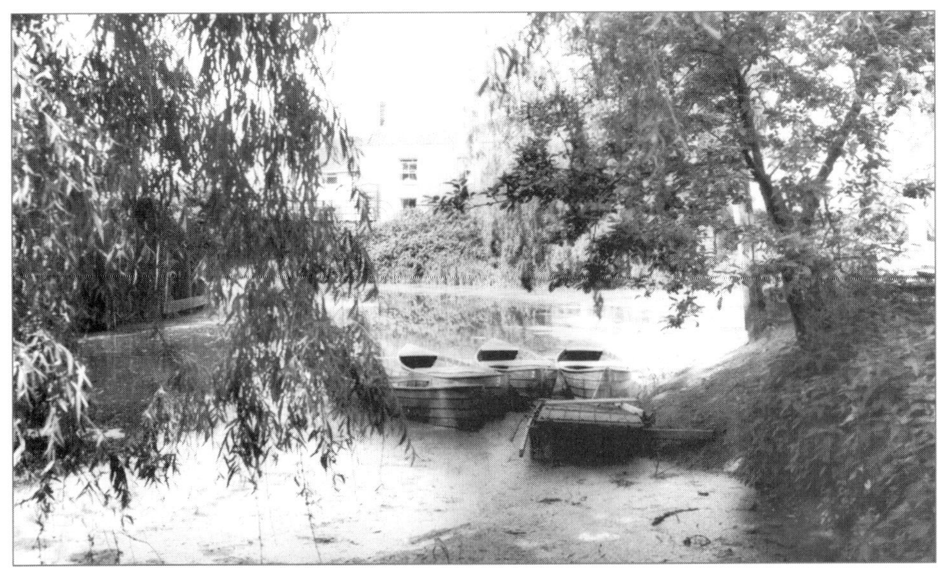

OUTWELL
Well Creek c1965
O79013

Outwell and Upwell are named after the Great Well Stream, which was formerly an important river for navigation, running down to Wisbech. There was once a wharf and tramway siding here. As in many Fenland streams, the water level is higher than the surrounding land: the Well Creek is actually carried over the Middle Level Drain, which was cut in 1848.

OUTWELL, *Beaupre Primary School c1965* O79003

This school opened in 1939 for infants and junior children. It is named after the Beaupre family, lords of the manor here for several centuries. There is still a Beaupre Hall in the village and Beaupre family tombs in the parish church.

▼ **OUTWELL,** *St Andrew's Methodist Church c1965* O79002

Nonconformity was a strong force in many Fenland villages, with Primitive Methodism especially influential from the 1820s. This church was very new at the time of the photograph: it was built in 1962, replacing the Victorian Wesleyan and Primitive chapels in the town.

▶ **TEN MILE BANK**
c1955 T225005

The Ten Mile Bank represents an early attempt to increase the flow of water in the river Ouse by straightening its course. The bank is to the right of the photograph, and the level of the water in the river behind it is well above the land on which the houses are built. This means that excess water has to be pumped up into the river to flow away.

◄ DOWNHAM MARKET
The Town Hall c1965 D149008

The Town Hall was built in 1887; the architect was J J Johnson. It is dominated by its square tower, and its steeply pitched roof has a Dutch-style gable. The large building opposite is the British Rifleman inn.

► DOWNHAM MARKET,
The Memorial c1965 D149036

This memorial has a Gothic-style pinnacle rather than a cross. Some people thought that a cross was not an appropriate symbol on a war memorial, as the dead could include people of all faiths and of none. The building to its left is occupied by Long's, a stonemasons.

DOWNHAM MARKET
The Clock Tower c1965 D149010

This was taken at the same time as D149008, as we can see from the
identical position of the cars. The clock tower is of cast iron, built in
1878; the designer was William Cunliffe.

DENVER
Denver Sluice c1965 D149005

Denver Sluice is the heart of Vermuyden's fen drainage plan. It prevents high tides coming further up the Ouse, and also controls excess river water coming downstream. It was first built in 1652, but collapsed under the pressure of the water in 1713. It was rebuilt in 1752 and has been enlarged several times since.

DENVER, *The Mill c1960* D211049a

This mill was not used for drainage, but for grinding corn; it was built for John Porter in 1835. It is of six storeys, with four sails and a fantail to turn the cap so that the sails are in the right position to pick up the wind.

THE CAMBRIDGESHIRE FENS

The Cambridgeshire Fens stretch from Tydd in the north almost to Cambridge in the south. The area around Wisbech is classic fenland, as flat as a table. There are many places of interest, including the port of Wisbech itself, inland ports like Burwell and Waterbeach, and March with its wonderful church. The only area of 'natural' fenland that survives is in Cambridgeshire, at Wicken Fen.

WISBECH, *The Clarkson Memorial 1901* 47583

This memorial was designed by George Gilbert Scott. It commemorates Thomas Clarkson, born in Wisbech in 1760. He dedicated his life to the abolition of slavery, and lived to see the passing of the Emancipation Bill of 1833. The houses behind the memorial are on the far side of the river Nene.

WISBECH, *Leach's Mill 1929* 81981

The roller mills are dominated by the former windmill, eight storeys high. This was one of the few windmills to have had eight sails. One sail blew off in a great storm in 1885 and landed in Town Park. The other sails were taken down two years later.

WISBECH, *High Street 1929* 81966

Awnings are out on the sunny side of the street. The Rose and Crown is an 18th-century building, but it has Tudor cellars underneath. Wisbech inns did not always have the highest reputation: John Byng wrote about his visit in 1790 'my horses could not eat the hay and I could not drink the wine'.

WISBECH
The Market 1929 81975

Market inns line the right hand side of the square - the Griffin, the
Ship Hotel and the Mermaid Inn. The market stalls include an ice
cream salesman (centre foreground) immediately in front of the
steps leading down to the ladies' convenience!

WISBECH
The Canal 1929 81972

The success of Wisbech has always depended on its rivers and
canals; indeed, it is named after the Wis Beck or stream. The canal
was built in the late 1790s. It reached the main river opposite the
Ship Defiance inn, just visible beyond the bridge (right).

LEVERINGTON
The Church c1960
L451005

The church is dedicated to St Leonard. Mid-Lent Sunday was known in Leverington as Whirling Sunday. This derives from a legend that a widow baking cakes on that day was snatched up by the devil in a whirlwind; she flew right over the tower of this church, and was never seen again!

LEVERINGTON, *Church Street c1960* L451003

Recent houses contrast with the thatched cottage on the right. The mini must have been a very new car when this photograph was taken: it was first produced in August 1959. Quiet Leverington has one claim to fame: Oliver Goldsmith is supposed to have written his play 'She Stoops to Conquer' here and to have based the Lumpkin character on a local farmer.

▼ **ELM,** *The Village 1923* 73583

Here we see a traditional village war memorial, a Cross of Sacrifice on an eight-sided base.
The form is similar to that of many on the First World War battlefields. The names on the
Elm memorial include that of local boy Charles Barker, reported killed in action in France on
21 August 1915: he was just fifteen years old.

▶ **MARCH**

*St Wendreda's Church
1929* 81922

This church has a fine spire,
but it is noted above all for
the wonderful carpentry of
its roof. More than a
hundred angels adorn the
double hammer beam
design. The poet John
Betjeman said that it was
'worth cycling 40 miles into
a headwind to see'.

MARCH
The Bridge from Nene Quay 1929
81913

Here we see leisure activity on the river Nene. The clock tower of the Town Hall is prominent. The Town Hall opened in 1900; the architect was W T Unwin. The row of shops facing the river include that of A Crowson, 'fancy goods dealer'.

MARCH
Looking Towards the Bridge 1929
81911

The trees in the centre of the photograph are the ones standing on the left bank of the Nene that we can see in 81913. The café on the right boasts an advertising sign for Hovis Bread, one of the most common advertisements found in English market towns.

MARCH
The War Memorial and Broad Street 1929 81906

The memorial portrays a soldier, head bowed, rifle pointed to the ground. The names include that of Edward Adkinson, one of four people killed when the airship C25 was lost off Aberdeen in July 1918. To the right of the memorial is a row called Broadway Buildings, occupied by J B Levett, 'ladies' and gents' outfitters'.

MARCH
High Street c1955 M28013

We are looking towards the Market Place, with the Town Hall again
predominant. Thirsty traders have their needs catered for by
inns like the Royal Exchange (centre left) and Ye Olde Griffin
(centre right), any 'olde' features of which have been hidden by
the rendering.

CHATTERIS
High Street c1955 C210011

We can just see the pediment and upper storey of the grandest
house in town, the early 19th-century Chatteris House on the left,
behind the White Lion Inn. The street lighting, with its prefabricated
concrete posts, must have been a recent addition to the street scene.

CHATTERIS, *High Street c1955* C210003

A solitary cyclist is the only sign of life in this early evening scene. There was already a conflict between the cyclist and the motor car: the newspaper billboard reads 'Cyclist's death was accidental', a recollection of some local tragedy.

WHITTLESEY, *Market Place 1904* 51561

The Butter Cross was built in the late 17th century. There are two parish churches in Whittlesey, less than a quarter of a mile apart - St Andrew's and St Mary's. The stately spire of St Mary's is the one we see in this photograph.

WHITTLESEY
The Memorial c1965
W90015

This is another statue memorial, but unlike the one at March, the image is an allegorical one: a figure in armour rather than in khaki holds a long sword, not a rifle. The names on the memorial include six people with the local surname Anker, including three brothers, Bertie, Ernest and Fred.

LITTLEPORT
Main Street c1955
L366010

Note the sign for the Globe Inn (centre). It was here that the Littleport bread riots began on 22 May 1816. Local people gathered in protest at starvation wages and atrocious working conditions. They robbed farmers, and marched to Ely in protest. On their return they were cornered in the George Inn. They were tried at Ely: many were transported to Australia, and five were publicly hanged.

LITTLEPORT, *The River c1955* L366006

A dredging barge is towed along the Great Ouse. The vital importance of maintaining the banks of Fenland rivers can clearly be seen in this photograph: notice how far below the level of the river are the houses on the extreme right. The men who carried out the drainage work were known locally as 'Fen Slodgers'.

SUTTON
The Village and the Church c1955 S674001

The tower culminates in a double octagon, obviously inspired by the one at Ely Cathedral. Inside the church, a bench runs along the wall for the use of those who could not stand throughout the lengthy services of the Middle Ages; benches like this gave rise to the saying 'the weakest go to the wall'. Note the steep slope to the right of the church - a rare sight in Fenland!

SOHAM, *High Street c1955* S597009

Here we see another soldier memorial, like the one at March. The names of those killed in the Second World War have been added around the base of the monument. They include the names of several Soham men who died in captivity in the Far East following the capture of Singapore by the Japanese in 1942.

▶ SOHAM
From the Church Tower c1955
S597003

Soham owes its survival to the heroism of two local men, Ben Gimbert and Jim Nightall. On 2 June 1944, engine driver Gimbert noticed that the front wagon of his ammunition train was on fire. He and his fireman Nightall detached the wagon and pushed it into a cutting, so that the earth banks would smother the explosion. The wagon did explode: Nightall was killed and Gimbert badly injured, but the town was saved.

◀ SOHAM
The Church c1955 S597028

Few people know that there was once a cathedral at Soham, which was established by St Felix but destroyed by the Danes in the 9th century. The present church, dedicated to St Andrew, is a grand enough building, with its great west tower decorated with East Anglian flushwork at the top.

▲ **SOHAM,** *The Steelyard c1955* S597004

This is the centre of Soham, with the Fountain Inn on the corner and Lloyd's Bank beyond.
The curious machinery projecting from the weather-boarded building on the left is a device for
weighing loads on carts.

◄ **SOHAM**
*The Village College
c1960* S597031

Village colleges are unique to
Cambridgeshire. They act
both as schools and as
community centres for the
town and its surrounding
villages. They were the
creation of Henry Morris,
chief education officer of the
county for over 30 years
from 1922. He boasted: 'we
will lift the school leaving
age to 90'.

▲ **BURWELL**
High Street c1955 B728016

Burwell is a fen-edge settlement extending for 2 miles in a north/south direction. We can just see the church on the left, with its octagonal top and open lantern. The churchyard contains a memorial to 78 people who died together on 8 September 1727, when a barn in which they had gathered to watch a puppet show caught fire.

◀ **BURWELL**
The Windmill c1955 B728028

This is a typical fenland scene, with a huge sky forming the backdrop to a church spire or, as here, a windmill. The mill is built of local clunch stone; Burwell was the last place in England where clunch was quarried.

BURWELL, *The Lode c1955* B728003

The Old Lode is one of several canals built by the Romans and leading to the river Cam. The scene here is almost a timeless one, with the farm buildings reflected in the water.

WATERBEACH, *The Bridge Hotel, Clayhithe c1960* W509019

The name of the town does not refer to any beach, but comes from the Old English word 'beck', meaning 'stream'. Clayhithe was the harbour of Waterbeach; the word 'hythe' means 'landing-place'.

CAMBRIDGE
MOTORBOAT CLUB

WATERBEACH
*The River Cam,
Clayhithe c1955*
W509003

By the time of this photograph, the former harbour had been given over to leisure activities. In the 17th century many people thought that the river Cam would dry up as a result of Vermuyden's drainage scheme; Cambridge university and the town both protested against the building of the Denver Sluice!

WATERBEACH, *The River Cam from the Weir c1955* W509008

The flow of water has been controlled at Waterbeach since Roman times, when a canal was built to connect the Cam to the Great Ouse; this is part of the Car Dyke, which extends all the way to Lincolnshire and is the first canal in Britain. It was probably built both to control flooding and to provide a route for the transport of grain.

WATERBEACH, *Bottisham Locks, the River Cam c1955* W509009

The greatest skating race in Fenland history took place here in 1895. The competitors started at this lock, raced to Ely and back - and then back into Ely. Although the total distance was 30 miles, the result was a dead-heat!

SWAVESEY, *The Church 1898* 41295

Swavesey church is dedicated to St Andrew; it was restored in 1867 at the expense of Mrs Dudley Ryder. There is a beautiful monument inside to Anne Kempe, Lady Cutt, who died in 1631: two life-size angels hold open two stone doors.

SWAVESEY, *The Cobblestones c1965* S675009

It is hard now to imagine that Swavesey was an important town in the Middle Ages, with a market and a fair. Mare Fen in Swavesey was held to be the best place in the whole of Fenland for skating in Victorian times - world skating championships were even held here!

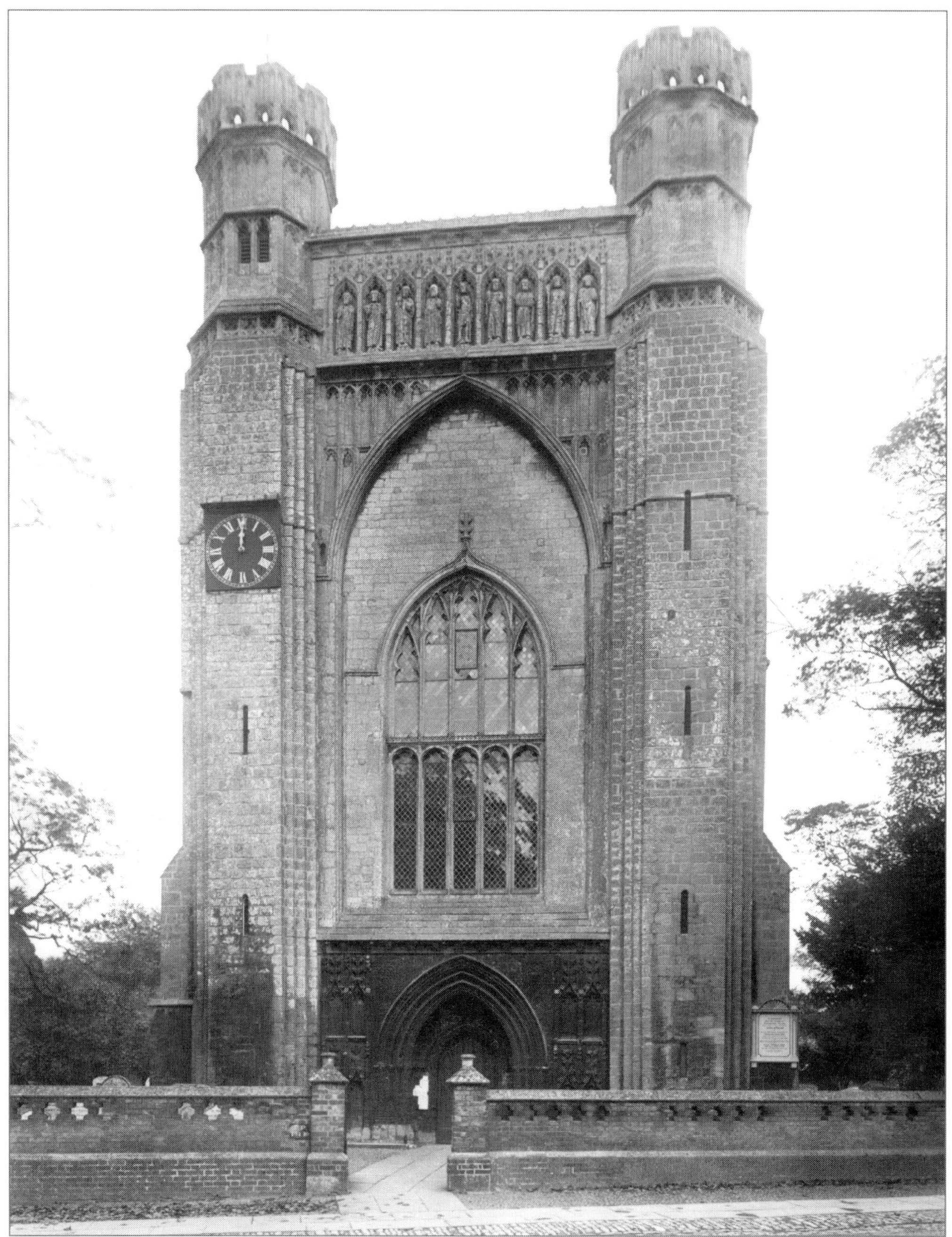

THORNEY, *The Abbey Church 1894* 34834

This grand-looking building is actually just a small part of the abbey church, which, like all the monasteries mentioned in this book, was dissolved by King Henry VIII in the 1530s. The Cambridge colleges of Trinity and Christ's College then plundered the site, taking away over 200 tons of stone. Inigo Jones converted what was left into Thorney parish church in 1638.

THORNEY
The Village Green c1955 T33006

Thorney was an estate village owned by the Dukes of Bedford; they
provided many facilities for their tenants, including high-quality housing
- and also lectures for those tenants who wished to improve themselves!

PETERBOROUGH AND THE FENS OF OLD HUNTINGDONSHIRE

PETERBOROUGH has expanded massively in the last 150 years, and it no longer has the feel of a Fenland town. However, its origin is the same as that of many towns in this book. It began as an early Saxon monastery that was destroyed by the Danes but re-founded well before the Norman Conquest. This monastery was dedicated to St Peter, and the borough or town that built up around it naturally took the name of Peterborough. The town is the best place from which to explore the Huntingdonshire fens; Ramsey Abbey and its estates, which included the town of St Ives with one of the largest fairs in medieval England, made up the heart of the area.

PETERBOROUGH
The Cathedral from the South-East 1890 24436

This photograph shows clearly the rounded east end of the Norman cathedral. The single-storey building to its right was added in the 16th century, but it is still known as 'The New Work'. It has a magnificent fan-vaulted ceiling. The crossing tower once had a wooden octagon like that at Ely, but it was rebuilt in the 1880s.

PETERBOROUGH
Long Causeway 1904 51549

Here we have a rear view of a tram very similar to that in 51550
(page 79), with the central street furniture serving a dual purpose as
streetlights and as supports for the tram wires. The large building on
the extreme right is Paten and Co, wine and spirits merchants.

PETERBOROUGH
Westgate 1904 51550

The street name has nothing to do with a town gate, but comes from
the Danish word 'gata', meaning street. This is a lasting legacy of the
relatively brief Danish occupation of this area. The ladies in the cart
(left) along with the handcart (centre right) suggest a leisurely age,
which is being rudely interrupted by the clang of the 'modern' tramcar.

PETERBOROUGH,
Church Street 1919 69092

Horse transport and bicycles dominate Church Street in this scene. This was formerly the heart of the town and its market place. The church of St John (right) was built as the parish church of Peterborough in the 15th century, incorporating stone from two earlier churches.

PETERBOROUGH,
Church Street c1955 P47048

Thirty-five years have passed since 69092 was taken, and the dominance of motor transport is obvious. However, the buildings are in many ways unchanged, including the rather insecure looking church clock. There are a few changes, however, including the two standard red telephone boxes visible behind the van on the right.

PETERBOROUGH
The Fountain 1919
69100

The cathedral authorities ran Peterborough until 1874, when a mayor and corporation was established. The first mayor was Henry Pearson Gates, and he served in the office a further four times. The fountain is a monument to him. It originally stood in front of the Butter Cross, from where this photograph was taken. In the 1960s the fountain was moved to the gardens in Bishop's Road.

PETERBOROUGH, *The Butter Cross 1890* 24451

This building has had many names since it was erected in 1670. It was then known as the Chamber over the Cross. In 1874 it became the town hall for the new Corporation. A few years later the name was changed to the Guild Hall. However, locals still call it by the name of the structure that was here even before 1670 - the Butter Cross.

► **RAMSEY**
*The Abbey
Gateway c1955*
R359004

An isolated abbey like Ramsey needed strong defences. In 1143 the marauding baron Geoffrey de Mandeville and his men occupied the abbey and held it against the king. The monks only got it back after Mandeville was killed the following year.

◄ **RAMSEY**
The Abbey c1955
R359011

This grand house was originally the home of the Fellowes family; they were the largest landowners in Huntingdonshire in the late 19th century, owning almost 16,000 acres in the county. At the time of this photograph, Ramsey Grammar School occupied the house.

▲ **RAMSEY,** *The Great Whyte c1955* R359023

In the Middle Ages a stream ran down the centre of the Great Whyte, and beer was delivered by boat to the many public houses here. We can see one pub, the White Swan, on the left, just behind the double-decker bus. The clock is a memorial to Edward Fellowes of Ramsey Abbey: it was erected in 1888.

◀ **WARBOYS**
The Church 1898 41293

The church is noted for its spire, which has very prominent openings. The church is dedicated to St Mary Magdalene, and is built of local cobblestone. The chancel to the right was rebuilt in brick in 1832.

WARBOYS
The Jubilee Clock and the Square c1955 W508010

The clock tower and the houses behind are of brick, probably produced locally: Warboys has been a centre for brick making since the late 19th century. On top of the weather vane (not visible in this photograph) is an image of a witch with a broomstick, commemorating the three alleged witches of Warboys who were hanged in 1593.

SOMERSHAM, *The Church 1898* 41294

This church has a very different feel to the one at Warboys, because only a small needle spire crowns its tower. Somersham with its church was at the centre of a very large Anglo-Saxon estate, or soke. The churches in surrounding villages were in fact chapels of this 'mother church'.

SOMERSHAM
The Cross c1955
S672015

There has been a market at Somersham since 1190, reflecting the importance of the town in the Middle Ages. We are looking along the High Street, with the George Inn on the left and the Rose and Crown on the right. Note the use of the telephone wires to support an overhead streetlight.

BLUNTISHAM, *High Street c1955* B726015

We can see the spire of the village church in the distance (left); the crime writer Dorothy L Sayers was brought up in the rectory. The structure in the centre of the road supports a weather vane as well as direction signs. Within the pillars is a barograph, a device that records changes in air pressure.

▶ **ST IVES**
*Market Square
1898* 41279

The spire on the left belongs to the Free Church of 1863; the architect was John Tarring. Public houses include the Robin Hood on the left and on the opposite side, the Cross Keys, immediately to the right of Thorpe's the 'Cash Drapery Stores'. The gable end advertises Wilson's, another tailor's.

▶ **ST IVES**
Bridge Street 1914
66957

We are looking from the bridge. The first house on the left is the Manor House. It has been 'restored' with a treatment of half-timbering since photograph 41276. Note the extremely tall telegraph poles: St Ives was clearly about to embrace the telephone in a major way!

▼ **ST IVES,** *The Bridge 1898* 41276

Ramsey Abbey owned St Ives, and a bridge was built here as early as 1107. The present stone bridge dates from the 15th century, although the two arches at the left-hand end were rebuilt in the 18th century. The curious central feature is a chapel, one of only four bridge chapels remaining in England. The gabled building to the right is the Manor House.

► **ST IVES**
Market Place 1901
48068

This is one of several examples in this book of how photographs can capture change in the landscape. The new feature since 41279 is the statue of Oliver Cromwell (centre left), which gives a very different focus to the Market Place. Cromwell lived in St Ives from 1631 until 1636, when he moved to Ely.

BOSTON
AND THE
LINCOLNSHIRE FENS

THE KEY to the Lincolnshire fenland is Boston, one of the most important ports in England in the Middle Ages. It declined later, but revived in the 19th century. The tower of the parish church - the famous Boston Stump - is the tallest in England. Other towns in this region include Spalding, at its peak in Georgian times, and market towns such as Bourne, Holbeach and Long Sutton; villages like Revesby lie at the extreme northern edge of the Fens.

BOSTON *St Botolph's Church 1899* 43293

The height of the tower makes it hard to appreciate how large the church is. The monument (centre left) is to Herbert Ingram. He was born in Boston, and was the founder of the 'Illustrated London News'. He and his son were among 300 people drowned in a shipping collision on Lake Michigan in America in 1860.

▲ BOSTON,
St Botolph's Church 1899 43289

Boston is actually a shortened form of 'St Botolph's Stone': the saint founded a religious house here. The church tower rises dramatically from the edge of the Witham. Locals tell you that you can see New York from the top - there is a hamlet of that name about seven miles from Boston!

► BOSTON
St Botolph's Church, the Interior 1893 32069

The Victorian font leads the eye into the church. Monuments here reflect Boston's maritime history. There is one to Wisselus, a merchant from Munster in Germany, who died in Boston in 1312, and others to George Bass and Joseph Banks, who both sailed to the South Pacific with Captain Cook.

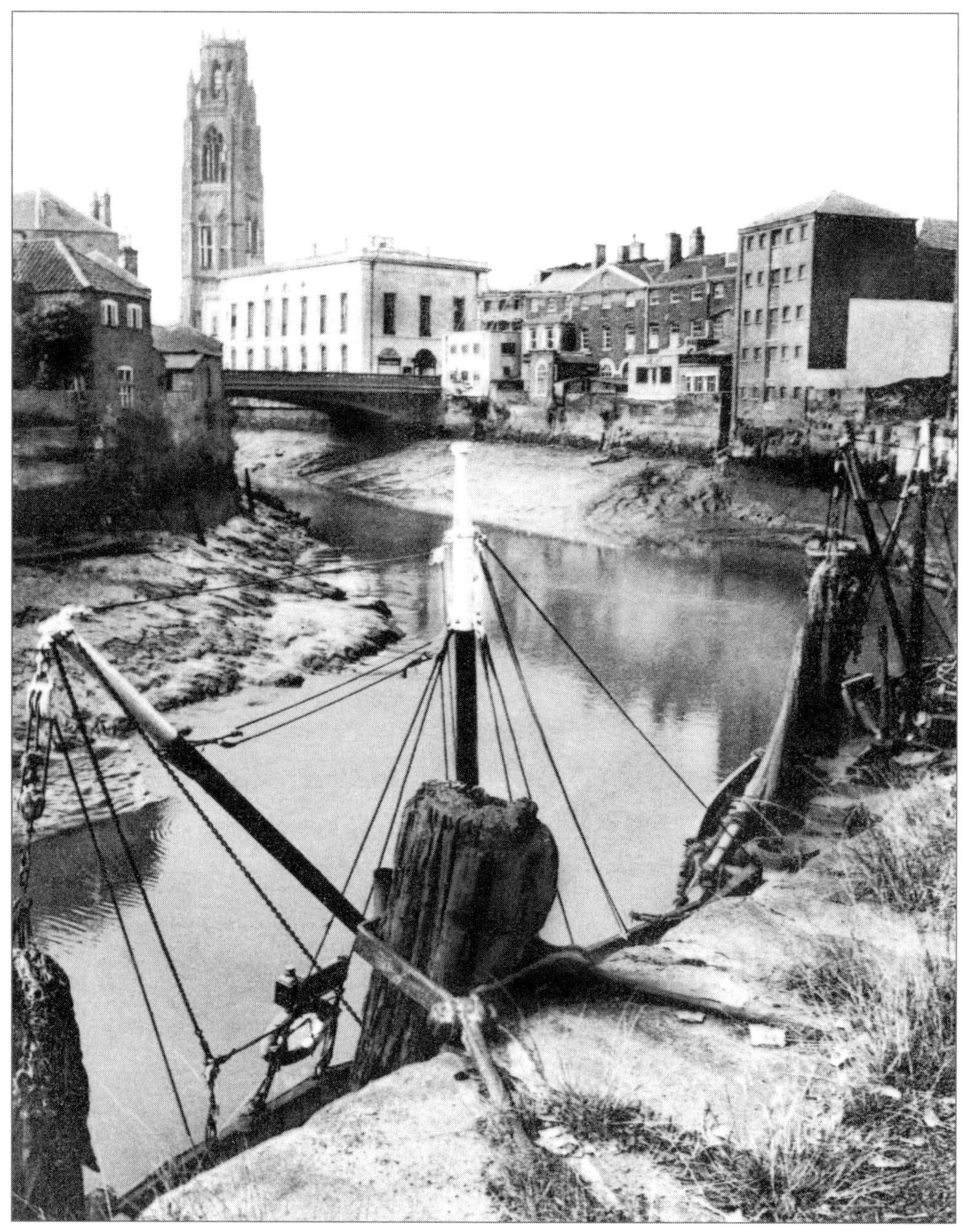

BOSTON
The Quay c1955 B155046

Here we see small local vessels moored at low tide beside a
neglected section of the quay, with the ever-present Stump beyond
rising to a height of 272 feet.

BOSTON, *The Sluice, the Bridge and the River c1955*   B155064

We are looking down from the Stump to the Grand Sluice. This was built in 1766, and was designed to allow water to flow downstream but prevent tidal water going further up the river. A lock provided for ships going upstream to Lincoln. The bridge behind carries the railway over the river Witham.

BOSTON
Shodfriars Hall
1889 22274

This was once thought to be largely a creation of the Victorian architect John Oldrid Scott. However, if you rid the house of the triangular gables, what remains is an excellent example of a large late medieval building, with two jettied storeys. It seems too big to be a merchant's house; perhaps it was a guildhall.

BOSTON

The Britannia c1965 B155088a

This is a waterfront watering-hole. Bateman's Brewery, with its well-known slogan 'Good Honest Ales', is one of the few local breweries to have retained its independence. It is based at Wainfleet, and was founded in 1874.

BOSTON

Doughty Quay 1890 26066

There is a wide range of water transport in this busy scene, including a paddle steamer, the 'Boston'. The boy at the top of the steps (left) is one-legged, like the man in the centre of 43295, page 99. These images remind us of the primitive nature of Victorian medicine: amputation was often the only cure for a diseased limb.

▲ **BOSTON**
The Docks 1893 32078

Boston Dock was constructed in 1881. It was partly paid for by the railway company who built a line to the dock: we can see a row of railway wagons on the quay to the left of the photograph. There are both sailing vessels and steamships moored here.

◄ **BOSTON**
The Docks c1955 B155009

Over sixty years have passed since 32078 was taken, and sail power has long gone from Boston Dock. The ship to the left is from Groningen in the Netherlands; in the 20th century, as in the Middle Ages, the North Sea was a highway for trade, not a barrier to communication.

BOSTON
The Theatre c1965 B155092

Friars were groups of priests who worked with the poor in urban areas, preaching and attending to their spiritual needs. In this book they appear only at Lynn and at Boston, the two great ports of the Fens. The building we see here is the dining room of the community of the Black Friars. At the time of the photograph it was used as a theatre: the billboard advertises the play 'The Rivals' by Sheridan.

BOSTON
The Windmill c1965 B155097

The mill was built in 1819 to grind grain brought here by barge. It is unusual in that it has five sails. It is known as the Maud Foster mill, after the canal or drain by which it stands. The drain itself was built in 1568: tradition says that Maud Foster owned the land through which it was built, and sold it on favourable terms provided that the drain preserved her name for ever!

BOSTON
The Sessions House 1893 32072

Battlements give this 1840s building an air of authority. Practical
security needs are not neglected, however: the window bars are of
iron, not wood! The architect was Charles Kirk senior.

BOSTON,
The Hospital 1899
43309

The Cottage Hospital in Boston opened in 1871; perhaps the amputees in 43295 and 26066 had their operations here. Although amputation seems a drastic operation, it was in fact a life-saver, preventing gangrene from spreading to the whole body with fatal results. A typical late Victorian perambulator stands by the bench.

BOSTON, *The Bath Gardens 1893* 32075

There were baths in Boston - using sea-water - from 1835, but the title refers to the Baths built here by the Corporation in 1879. Eight years earlier, the Corporation had established this beautiful park covering over 30 acres beside the river. It was the first 'People's Park' in Lincolnshire.

◄**BOSTON**
The Cemetery 1899
43306

Cemeteries were founded in many towns in the 1850s, because churchyards had become unhealthily overcrowded and were blamed for the spread of cholera. This cemetery was laid out on 12 acres of land north of the town. Herbert Ingram (see 43293, page 88) is buried here, his body having been brought back from America; his son's body was never found.

▲ BOSTON
Market Place 1899 43295

It is market day, and the town is busy. Many inns, including the Rum Puncheon and the Angel Hotel (to the left and right of the church) provide refreshment. Behind the gas-lamp on the right is a typically Victorian institution - Lammie's Temperance Hotel.

► BOSTON
The Market Place c1955
B155054

Half a century after 43295 was taken, the cobbled surface has been replaced by asphalt and the motor coach has arrived. The great height of the stump shows well in this photograph.

BOSTON
Market Place c1950
B155005

Here we have another mid 20th-century image, this time looking away from the church. Note the reassuring presence of the bobby on his beat (right). The Victorian Gothic building on the extreme left is occupied by the Boston Gas Light Company.

FRAMPTON, *The Fishbourne Inn Tea Gardens c1960* F148018

The inn sign under the tree advertises Mew's Ales. Frampton is situated just south of Boston, and it is a very pleasant spot for walking and cycling; the marsh around the Wash, beyond the medieval sea-wall, is a paradise for bird watchers.

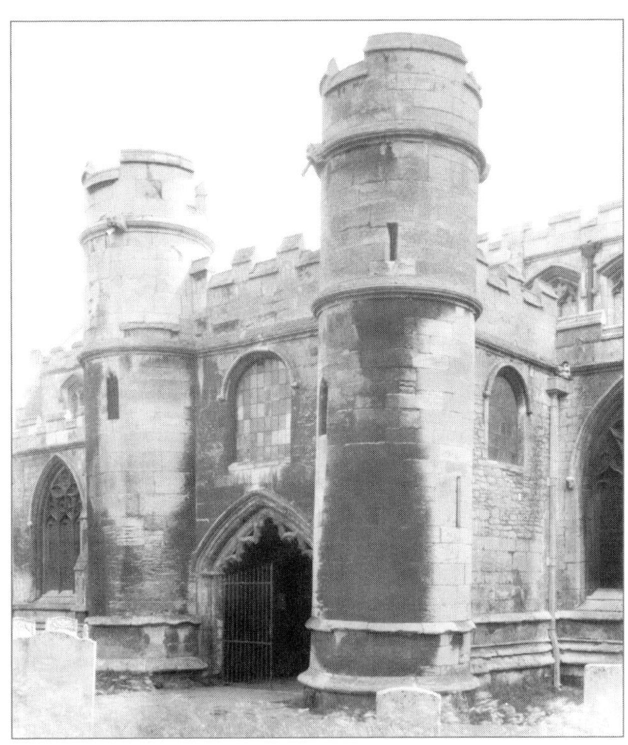

▶ HOLBEACH
*All Saints' Parish Church,
the North Door c1955* H318030

It is not known when these unique turrets were added to the porch; it is not even known whether they were built for the porch, or if they came from a castle - if they did, Moulton Castle would seem the most likely source.

▼ HOLBEACH
High Street c1955 H318015

The 180ft-tall spire of the parish church is visible in the background of this scene, taken just after school has closed – note the girls in sports uniform and carrying tennis rackets on the right. Behind Barclay's Bank (left) is the start of Albert Street; this part of the town was developed in the years after 1840, when Queen Victoria married Prince Albert.

HOLBEACH
Carters Park c1965 H318064

This is a closely mown park: one would hardly dare to walk on the
grass here! The park is named after H P Carter, who lived at Stukeley
Hall in the early 20th century and donated 10 acres of open space to
the town. The park gates celebrate the coronation of Queen
Elizabeth in 1953.

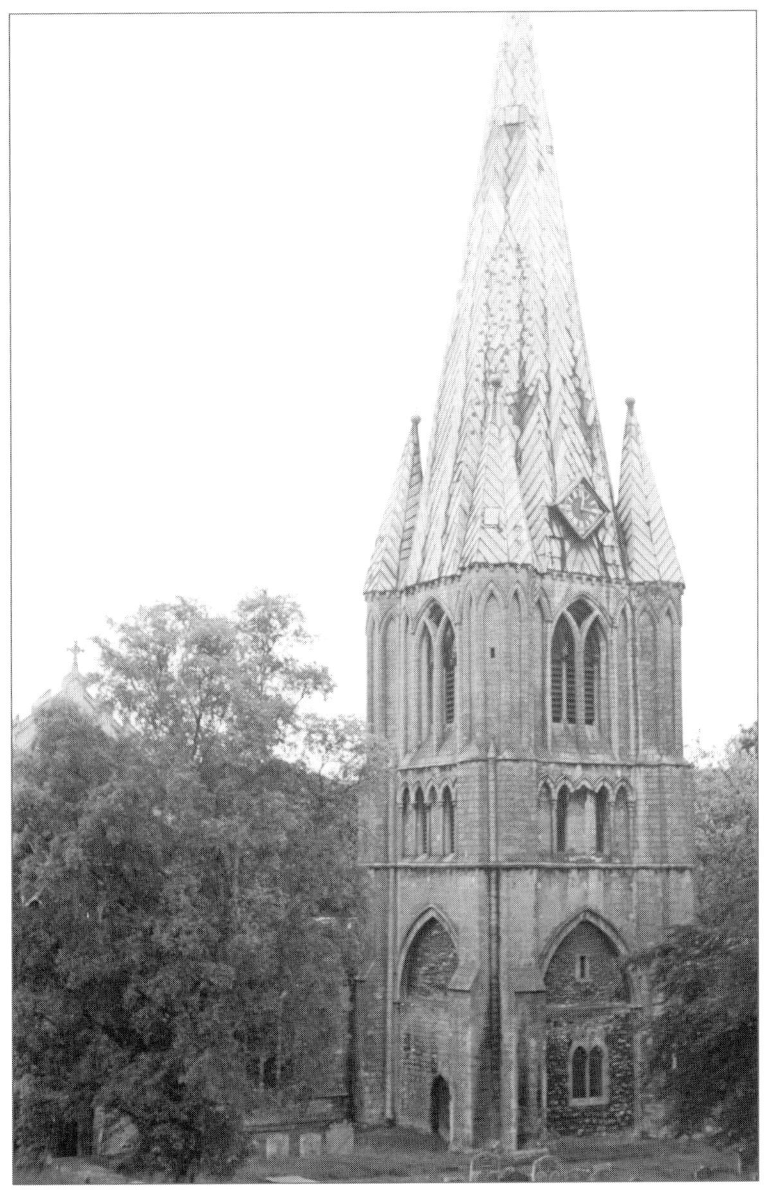

LONG SUTTON
The Church c1950 L484003

The spire with its leaning-in turrets is one of the most unusual in
England. It is made of wood entirely covered with lead. The ground
floor of the tower was once open to the elements: we can clearly see
the later infilling of the tall arches.

▲ LONG SUTTON
Market Place c1960 L484011

Here we see the Market Place on a quiet day: there is plenty of space for fairly haphazard parking of assorted forms of vehicles! Dick Turpin lived at Long Sutton in 1737, under the name of John Palmer, selling horses that he had probably stolen; he lived at the Bull (centre) for a while, and then in a cottage in the High Street.

► LONG SUTTON
The Park c1955 L484023

Autumn leaves lie on the grass of a park much less formal than the one at Holbeach. Parks like this make up the lungs of a town, allowing space for quiet reflection.

CROWLAND, *The Abbey c1965* C198043

The abbey is on the site of a hermitage founded by St Guthlac; it stood on an island in the Fens at that time. The villagers used the north aisle of the abbey church as their parish church. When the abbey was dissolved, the buildings were destroyed, but the parish church was still used, so that the church now stands among the abbey ruins.

CROWLAND, *The Abbey Hostel c1965* C198034

We can see the tower at the west end of the parish church, with the west end of the abbey adjoining it. There would once have been a triangular gable rising over the abbey window; the statue of Christ now on Crowland Bridge may have come from here. The Abbey Hostel inn is on the right.

CROWLAND
The Bridge 1894
34833

The unique triangular bridge now crosses over nothing! This is a good example of man-made changes to the landscape in the Fens: the rivers Nene and Welland once met beneath these arches, but they have long been diverted. This was an important spot once: monarchs landed here to visit the abbey.

DEEPING ST JAMES, *The Church and the Cross c1965* D150001

The church spire, unlike most others in this book, is not medieval: it was built in about 1717. In the foreground is the village cross. It once held a tall shaft, but this was taken down in 1819 when the base was converted into the village lock-up. Inside there are three stone seats with chains.

SPALDING
High Bridge c1960 S388227

Spalding is built along both sides of the river Welland, like a town in
the Netherlands. Many towns have a road by-pass, but Spalding has
a river by-pass: the narrow river through the town led to flooding as
water built up behind it, so a channel was built around the town to
carry off this excess water.

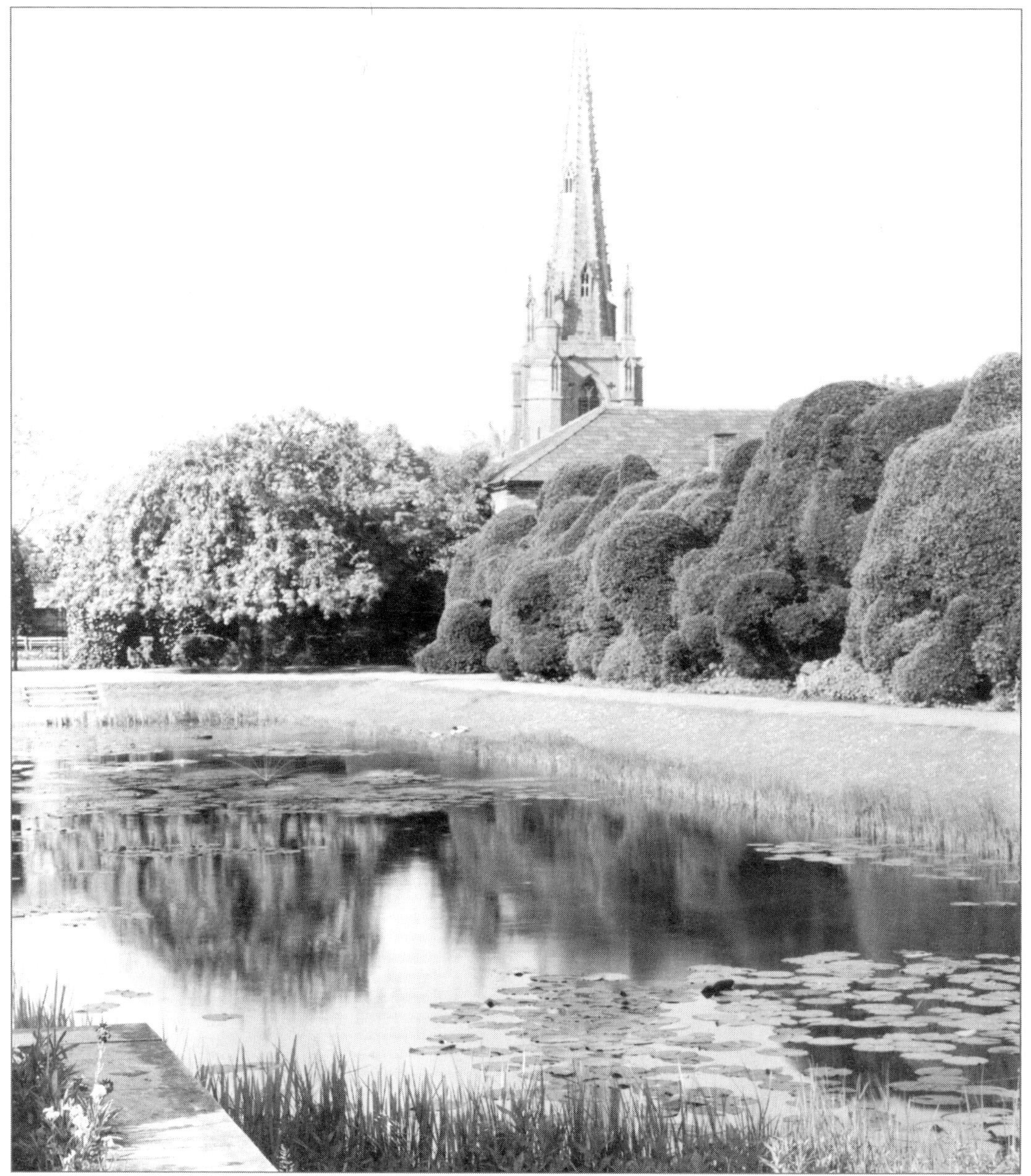

SPALDING
The Church c1955 S388145

We are in the grounds of Ayscoughfee Hall – we can see its roof behind the
trees (centre). The gardens were laid out in 1730. This lily pond is just in front
of Lutyens' war memorial of 1925. The tall spire of the parish church of St
Mary and St Nicholas dominates the view: it is 160 feet high.

SPALDING, *Market Place c1955* S388171

It is market day. To the left are the market inns, the early 19th-century Red Lion Hotel and the 18th-century White Hart Hotel. Both have porches extending across the pavement.

▶ **SPALDING**
Sheep Market c1955 S388156

The white building on the right is the Prior's Oven café. This is an octagonal room, and is supposed to have been part of the medieval priory of Spalding; one tradition says that it was the priory prison!

BOURNE, *The Swimming Pool c1955* B511010

Smiling faces around the pool give the lie to the claim that Bourne is the coldest place in the Fens. The town is known for the high quality of its water. In the early 20th century, Mills and Baxter were one of the town's largest employers, making a dozen varieties of fizzy drinks; they obtained their water from a bore-hole in North Street.

BOURNE, *The Church c1955* B511007

Bourne is the westernmost town in this book, and its position at the edge of the Fens is reflected in the number of trees in the photograph. The church is dedicated to St Peter and St Paul, and was once a house of Augustinian canons; it is one of the few monastic churches surviving in Lincolnshire.

BOURNE
North Street 1952 .

Bourne's market place is at the heart of the town, with streets
radiating from it in all directions. This is North Street. To the
right Lloyd's Bank have built themselves a mock-Tudor
building, while on the left the Midland Bank is content to
occupy a pre-existing building.

▲ DONINGTON
The Queen Inn c1965 D220024

S&P (on the central gable of the inn) stands for Steward and Patteson, one of the four great breweries of Norwich. They acquired many pubs in Lincolnshire by mergers and take-overs, including East Anglian Breweries of Ely and Huntingdon. The Watney Mann empire swallowed up Steward and Patteson itself in 1963.

◄ DONINGTON
The Old Mill Pit c1965 D220042

A timeless scene, but the cart is of course a conscious recreation of the past. Donington is a small market town, with a school founded by Thomas Cowley in 1719. The explorer Matthew Flinders is buried in Donington church.

DONINGTON
The Church c1955 D220019

The church has an unusual dedication, St Mary and the Holy Rood. The rood is the cross on which Jesus was crucified, and there was probably once a fragment of it in this church - an object of veneration and pilgrimage. The tower here was originally detached from the church.

REVESBY
The Church R306001

The most northerly village in this book, Revesby is also the only
settlement in it with a name that has a Danish origin. The 18th- and
19th-century almshouses on the left are actually earlier than the
present church, which was built in 1890. The explorer and botanist
Joseph Banks was born at Revesby in 1743.

INDEX

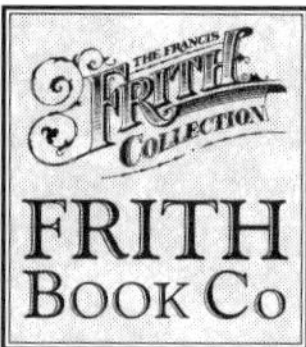

Frith Book Co Titles

www.francisfrith.co.uk

The Frith Book Company publishes over 100 new titles each year. A selection of those currently available are listed below. For latest catalogue please contact Frith Book Co.
Town Books 96 pages, approximately 100 photos. **County and Themed Books** 128 pages, approximately 150 photos (unless specified). All titles hardback with laminated case and jacket, except those indicated pb (paperback)

Amersham, Chesham & Rickmansworth (pb)	1-85937-340-2	£9.99	Devon (pb)	1-85937-297-x	£9.99
Andover (pb)	1-85937-292-9	£9.99	Devon Churches (pb)	1-85937-250-3	£9.99
Aylesbury (pb)	1-85937-227-9	£9.99	Dorchester (pb)	1-85937-307-0	£9.99
Barnstaple (pb)	1-85937-300-3	£9.99	Dorset (pb)	1-85937-269-4	£9.99
Basildon Living Memories (pb)	1-85937-515-4	£9.99	Dorset Coast (pb)	1-85937-299-6	£9.99
Bath (pb)	1-85937-419-0	£9.99	Dorset Living Memories (pb)	1-85937-584-7	£9.99
Bedford (pb)	1-85937-205-8	£9.99	Down the Severn (pb)	1-85937-560-x	£9.99
Bedfordshire Living Memories	1-85937-513-8	£14.99	Down The Thames (pb)	1-85937-278-3	£9.99
Belfast (pb)	1-85937-303-8	£9.99	Down the Trent	1-85937-311-9	£14.99
Berkshire (pb)	1-85937-191-4	£9.99	East Anglia (pb)	1-85937-265-1	£9.99
Berkshire Churches	1-85937-170-1	£17.99	East Grinstead (pb)	1-85937-138-8	£9.99
Berkshire Living Memories	1-85937-332-1	£14.99	East London	1-85937-080-2	£14.99
Black Country	1-85937-497-2	£12.99	East Sussex (pb)	1-85937-606-1	£9.99
Blackpool (pb)	1-85937-393-3	£9.99	Eastbourne (pb)	1-85937-399-2	£9.99
Bognor Regis (pb)	1-85937-431-x	£9.99	Edinburgh (pb)	1-85937-193-0	£8.99
Bournemouth (pb)	1-85937-545-6	£9.99	England In The 1880s	1-85937-331-3	£17.99
Bradford (pb)	1-85937-204-x	£9.99	Essex - Second Selection	1-85937-456-5	£14.99
Bridgend (pb)	1-85937-386-0	£7.99	Essex (pb)	1-85937-270-8	£9.99
Bridgwater (pb)	1-85937-305-4	£9.99	Essex Coast	1-85937-342-9	£14.99
Bridport (pb)	1-85937-327-5	£9.99	Essex Living Memories	1-85937-490-5	£14.99
Brighton (pb)	1-85937-192-2	£8.99	Exeter	1-85937-539-1	£9.99
Bristol (pb)	1-85937-264-3	£9.99	Exmoor (pb)	1-85937-608-8	£9.99
British Life A Century Ago (pb)	1-85937-213-9	£9.99	Falmouth (pb)	1-85937-594-4	£9.99
Buckinghamshire (pb)	1-85937-200-7	£9.99	Folkestone (pb)	1-85937-124-8	£9.99
Camberley (pb)	1-85937-222-8	£9.99	Frome (pb)	1-85937-317-8	£9.99
Cambridge (pb)	1-85937-422-0	£9.99	Glamorgan	1-85937-488-3	£14.99
Cambridgeshire (pb)	1-85937-420-4	£9.99	Glasgow (pb)	1-85937-190-6	£9.99
Cambridgeshire Villages	1-85937-523-5	£14.99	Glastonbury (pb)	1-85937-338-0	£7.99
Canals And Waterways (pb)	1-85937-291-0	£9.99	Gloucester (pb)	1-85937-232-5	£9.99
Canterbury Cathedral (pb)	1-85937-179-5	£9.99	Gloucestershire (pb)	1-85937-561-8	£9.99
Cardiff (pb)	1-85937-093-4	£9.99	Great Yarmouth (pb)	1-85937-426-3	£9.99
Carmarthenshire (pb)	1-85937-604-5	£9.99	Greater Manchester (pb)	1-85937-266-x	£9.99
Chelmsford (pb)	1-85937-310-0	£9.99	Guildford (pb)	1-85937-410-7	£9.99
Cheltenham (pb)	1-85937-095-0	£9.99	Hampshire (pb)	1-85937-279-1	£9.99
Cheshire (pb)	1-85937-271-6	£9.99	Harrogate (pb)	1-85937-423-9	£9.99
Chester (pb)	1-85937-382 8	£9.99	Hastings and Bexhill (pb)	1-85937-131-0	£9.99
Chesterfield (pb)	1-85937-378-x	£9.99	Heart of Lancashire (pb)	1-85937-197-3	£9.99
Chichester (pb)	1-85937-228-7	£9.99	Helston (pb)	1-85937-214-7	£9.99
Churches of East Cornwall (pb)	1-85937-249-x	£9.99	Hereford (pb)	1-85937-175-2	£9.99
Churches of Hampshire (pb)	1-85937-207-4	£9.99	Herefordshire (pb)	1-85937-567-7	£9.99
Cinque Ports & Two Ancient Towns	1-85937-492-1	£14.99	Herefordshire Living Memories	1-85937-514-6	£14.99
Colchester (pb)	1-85937-188-4	£8.99	Hertfordshire (pb)	1-85937-247-3	£9.99
Cornwall (pb)	1-85937-229-5	£9.99	Horsham (pb)	1-85937-432-8	£9.99
Cornwall Living Memories	1-85937-248-1	£14.99	Humberside (pb)	1-85937-605-3	£9.99
Cotswolds (pb)	1-85937-230-9	£9.99	Hythe, Romney Marsh, Ashford (pb)	1-85937-256-2	£9.99
Cotswolds Living Memories	1-85937-255-4	£14.99	Ipswich (pb)	1-85937-424-7	£9.99
County Durham (pb)	1-85937-398-4	£9.99	Isle of Man (pb)	1-85937-268-6	£9.99
Croydon Living Memories (pb)	1-85937-162-0	£9.99	Isle of Wight (pb)	1-85937-429-8	£9.99
Cumbria (pb)	1-85937-621-5	£9.99	Isle of Wight Living Memories	1-85937-304-6	£14.99
Derby (pb)	1-85937-367-4	£9.99	Kent (pb)	1-85937-189-2	£9.99
Derbyshire (pb)	1-85937-196-5	£9.99	Kent Living Memories(pb)	1-85937-401-8	£9.99
Derbyshire Living Memories	1-85937-330-5	£14.99	Kings Lynn (pb)	1-85937-334-8	£9.99

Available from your local bookshop or from the publisher

Frith Book Co Titles (continued)

Title	ISBN	Price	Title	ISBN	Price
Lake District (pb)	1-85937-275-9	£9.99	Sherborne (pb)	1-85937-301-1	£9.99
Lancashire Living Memories	1-85937-335-6	£14.99	Shrewsbury (pb)	1-85937-325-9	£9.99
Lancaster, Morecambe, Heysham (pb)	1-85937-233-3	£9.99	Shropshire (pb)	1-85937-326-7	£9.99
Leeds (pb)	1-85937-202-3	£9.99	Shropshire Living Memories	1-85937-643-6	£14.99
Leicester (pb)	1-85937-381-x	£9.99	Somerset	1-85937-153-1	£14.99
Leicestershire & Rutland Living Memories	1-85937-500-6	£12.99	South Devon Coast	1-85937-107-8	£14.99
Leicestershire (pb)	1-85937-185-x	£9.99	South Devon Living Memories (pb)	1-85937-609-6	£9.99
Lighthouses	1-85937-257-0	£9.99	South East London (pb)	1-85937-263-5	£9.99
Lincoln (pb)	1-85937-380-1	£9.99	South Somerset	1-85937-318-6	£14.99
Lincolnshire (pb)	1-85937-433-6	£9.99	South Wales	1-85937-519-7	£14.99
Liverpool and Merseyside (pb)	1-85937-234-1	£9.99	Southampton (pb)	1-85937-427-1	£9.99
London (pb)	1-85937-183-3	£9.99	Southend (pb)	1-85937-313-5	£9.99
London Living Memories	1-85937-454-9	£14.99	Southport (pb)	1-85937-425-5	£9.99
Ludlow (pb)	1-85937-176-0	£9.99	St Albans (pb)	1-85937-341-0	£9.99
Luton (pb)	1-85937-235-x	£9.99	St Ives (pb)	1-85937-415-8	£9.99
Maidenhead (pb)	1-85937-339-9	£9.99	Stafford Living Memories (pb)	1-85937-503-0	£9.99
Maidstone (pb)	1-85937-391-7	£9.99	Staffordshire (pb)	1-85937-308-9	£9.99
Manchester (pb)	1-85937-198-1	£9.99	Stourbridge (pb)	1-85937-530-8	£9.99
Marlborough (pb)	1-85937-336-4	£9.99	Stratford upon Avon (pb)	1-85937-388-7	£9.99
Middlesex	1-85937-158-2	£14.99	Suffolk (pb)	1-85937-221-x	£9.99
Monmouthshire	1-85937-532-4	£14.99	Suffolk Coast (pb)	1-85937-610-x	£9.99
New Forest (pb)	1-85937-390-9	£9.99	Surrey (pb)	1-85937-240-6	£9.99
Newark (pb)	1-85937-366-6	£9.99	Surrey Living Memories	1-85937-328-3	£14.99
Newport, Wales (pb)	1-85937-258-9	£9.99	Sussex (pb)	1-85937-184-1	£9.99
Newquay (pb)	1-85937-421-2	£9.99	Sutton (pb)	1-85937-337-2	£9.99
Norfolk (pb)	1-85937-195-7	£9.99	Swansea (pb)	1-85937-167-1	£9.99
Norfolk Broads	1-85937-486-7	£14.99	Taunton (pb)	1-85937-314-3	£9.99
Norfolk Living Memories (pb)	1-85937-402-6	£9.99	Tees Valley & Cleveland (pb)	1-85937-623-1	£9.99
North Buckinghamshire	1-85937-626-6	£14.99	Teignmouth (pb)	1-85937-370-4	£7.99
North Devon Living Memories	1-85937-261-9	£14.99	Thanet (pb)	1-85937-116-7	£9.99
North Hertfordshire	1-85937-547-2	£14.99	Tiverton (pb)	1-85937-178-7	£9.99
North London (pb)	1-85937-403-4	£9.99	Torbay (pb)	1-85937-597-9	£9.99
North Somerset	1-85937-302-x	£14.99	Truro (pb)	1-85937-598-7	£9.99
North Wales (pb)	1-85937-298-8	£9.99	Victorian & Edwardian Dorset	1-85937-254-6	£14.99
North Yorkshire (pb)	1-85937-236-8	£9.99	Victorian & Edwardian Kent (pb)	1-85937-624-X	£9.99
Northamptonshire Living Memories	1-85937-529-4	£14.99	Victorian & Edwardian Maritime Album (pb)	1-85937-622-3	£9.99
Northamptonshire	1-85937-150-7	£14.99	Victorian and Edwardian Sussex (pb)	1-85937-625-8	£9.99
Northumberland Tyne & Wear (pb)	1-85937-281-3	£9.99	Villages of Devon (pb)	1-85937-293-7	£9.99
Northumberland	1-85937-522-7	£14.99	Villages of Kent (pb)	1-85937-294-5	£9.99
Norwich (pb)	1-85937-194-9	£8.99	Villages of Sussex (pb)	1-85937-295-3	£9.99
Nottingham (pb)	1-85937-324-0	£9.99	Warrington (pb)	1-85937-507-3	£9.99
Nottinghamshire (pb)	1-85937-187-6	£9.99	Warwick (pb)	1-85937-518-9	£9.99
Oxford (pb)	1-85937-411-5	£9.99	Warwickshire (pb)	1-85937-203-1	£9.99
Oxfordshire (pb)	1-85937-430-1	£9.99	Welsh Castles (pb)	1-85937-322-4	£9.99
Oxfordshire Living Memories	1-85937-525-1	£14.99	West Midlands (pb)	1-85937-289-9	£9.99
Paignton (pb)	1-85937-374-7	£7.99	West Sussex (pb)	1-85937-607-x	£9.99
Peak District (pb)	1-85937-280-5	£9.99	West Yorkshire (pb)	1-85937-201-5	£9.99
Pembrokeshire	1-85937-262-7	£14.99	Weston Super Mare (pb)	1-85937-306-2	£9.99
Penzance (pb)	1-85937-595-2	£9.99	Weymouth (pb)	1-85937-209-0	£9.99
Peterborough (pb)	1-85937-219-8	£9.99	Wiltshire (pb)	1-85937-277-5	£9.99
Picturesque Harbours	1-85937-208-2	£14.99	Wiltshire Churches (pb)	1-85937-171-x	£9.99
Piers	1-85937-237-6	£17.99	Wiltshire Living Memories (pb)	1-85937-396-8	£9.99
Plymouth (pb)	1-85937-389-5	£9.99	Winchester (pb)	1-85937-428-x	£9.99
Poole & Sandbanks (pb)	1-85937-251-1	£9.99	Windsor (pb)	1-85937-333-x	£9.99
Preston (pb)	1-85937-212-0	£9.99	Wokingham & Bracknell (pb)	1-85937-329-1	£9.99
Reading (pb)	1-85937-238-4	£9.99	Woodbridge (pb)	1-85937-498-0	£9.99
Redhill to Reigate (pb)	1-85937-596-0	£9.99	Worcester (pb)	1-85937-165-5	£9.99
Ringwood (pb)	1-85937-384-4	£7.99	Worcestershire Living Memories	1-85937-489-1	£14.99
Romford (pb)	1-85937-319-4	£9.99	Worcestershire	1-85937-152-3	£14.99
Royal Tunbridge Wells (pb)	1-85937-504-9	£9.99	York (pb)	1-85937-199-x	£9.99
Salisbury (pb)	1-85937-239-2	£9.99	Yorkshire (pb)	1-85937-186-8	£9.99
Scarborough (pb)	1-85937-379-8	£9.99	Yorkshire Coastal Memories	1-85937-506-5	£14.99
Sevenoaks and Tonbridge (pb)	1-85937-392-5	£9.99	Yorkshire Dales	1-85937-502-2	£14.99
Sheffield & South Yorks (pb)	1-85937-267-8	£9.99	Yorkshire Living Memories (pb)	1-85937-397-6	£9.99

See Frith books on the internet at www.francisfrith.co.uk

FRITH PRODUCTS & SERVICES

Francis Frith would doubtless be pleased to know that the pioneering publishing venture he started in 1860 still continues today. Over a hundred and forty years later, The Francis Frith Collection continues in the same innovative tradition and is now one of the foremost publishers of vintage photographs in the world. Some of the current activities include:

Interior Decoration

Today Frith's photographs can be seen framed and as giant wall murals in thousands of pubs, restaurants, hotels, banks, retail stores and other public buildings throughout the country. In every case they enhance the unique local atmosphere of the places they depict and provide reminders of gentler days in an increasingly busy and frenetic world.

Product Promotions

Frith products are used by many major companies to promote the sales of their own products or to reinforce their own history and heritage. Frith promotions have been used by Hovis bread, Courage beers, Scots Porage Oats, Colman's mustard, Cadbury's foods, Mellow Birds coffee, Dunhill pipe tobacco, Guinness, and Bulmer's Cider.

Genealogy and Family History

As the interest in family history and roots grows world-wide, more and more people are turning to Frith's photographs of Great Britain for images of the towns, villages and streets where their ancestors lived; and, of course, photographs of the churches and chapels where their ancestors were christened, married and buried are an essential part of every genealogy tree and family album.

Frith Products

All Frith photographs are available Framed or just as Mounted Prints and Posters (size 23 x 16 inches). These may be ordered from the address below. From time to time other products - Address Books, Calendars, Table Mats, etc - are available.

The Internet

Already fifty thousand Frith photographs can be viewed and purchased on the internet through the Frith websites and a myriad of partner sites.

For more detailed information on Frith companies and products, look at these sites:

www.francisfrith.co.uk
www.francisfrith.com
(for North American visitors)

See the complete list of Frith Books at:

www.francisfrith.co.uk

This web site is regularly updated with the latest list of publications from the Frith Book Company. If you wish to buy books relating to another part of the country that your local bookshop does not stock, you may purchase on-line.

For further information, trade, or author enquiries please contact us at the address below:
The Francis Frith Collection, Frith's Barn, Teffont, Salisbury, Wiltshire, England SP3 5QP.
Tel: +44 (0)1722 716 376 Fax: +44 (0)1722 716 881 Email: sales@francisfrith.co.uk

See Frith books on the internet at www.francisfrith.co.uk

HOW TO ORDER YOUR FREE MOUNTED PRINT
and other Frith prints at half price

Mounted Print
Overall size 14 x 11 inches

*Fill in and cut out this voucher and return it
with your remittance for £2.25 (to cover
postage and handling to UK addresses).
For overseas addresses please include £4.00
post and handling.
Choose any photograph included in this book.
Your SEPIA print will be A4 in size. It will be
mounted in a cream mount with a burgundy
rule line (overall size 14 x 11 inches).*

Order additional Mounted Prints
at HALF PRICE (only £7.49 each*)
If you would like to order more Frith prints
from this book, possibly as gifts for friends
and family, you can buy them at half price
(with no additional postage and handling
costs).

Have your Mounted Prints framed
For an extra £14.95 per print* you can have
your mounted print(s) framed in an elegant
polished wood and gilt moulding, overall
size 16 x 13 inches (no additional postage
and handling required).

---

* IMPORTANT!

**These special prices are only available if you
order at the same time as you order your free
mounted print. You must use the ORIGINAL
VOUCHER on this page (no copies permitted).
We can only despatch to one address.**

Voucher for **FREE** and Reduced Price *Frith Prints*

*Please do not photocopy this voucher. Only the original is valid,
so please fill it in, cut it out and return it to us with your order.*

Picture ref no	Page number	Qty	Mounted @ £7.49	Framed + £14.95	Total Cost
		1	Free of charge*	£	£
			£7.49	£	£
			£7.49	£	£
			£7.49	£	£
			£7.49	£	£
			£7.49	£	£
			£7.49	£	£

Please allow 28 days for delivery

* Post & handling (UK)	£2.25
Total Order Cost	£

Title of this book . . . .

I enclose a cheque/postal order for £ . . . .
made payable to 'The Francis Frith Collection'

OR please debit my Mastercard / Visa / Switch / Amex card
(credit cards please on all overseas orders), details below

Card Number

Issue No (Switch only)   Valid from (Amex/Switch)

Expires   Signature

Name Mr/Mrs/Ms ....

Address ....

....

....

.... Postcode ....

Daytime Tel No ....

Email ....

Valid to 31/12/05

Send completed Voucher form to:
The Francis Frith Collection, Frith's Barn, Teffont, Salisbury, Wiltshire SP3 5QP

Would you like to find out more about Francis Frith?

We have recently recruited some entertaining speakers who are happy to visit local groups, clubs and societies to give an illustrated talk documenting Frith's travels and photographs. If you are a member of such a group and are interested in hosting a presentation, we would love to hear from you.

Our speakers bring with them a small selection of our local town and county books, together with sample prints. They are happy to take orders. A small proportion of the order value is donated to the group who have hosted the presentation. The talks are therefore an excellent way of fundraising for small groups and societies.

Can you help us with information about any of the Frith photographs in this book?

We are gradually compiling an historical record for each of the photographs in the Frith archive. It is always fascinating to find out the names of the people shown in the pictures, as well as insights into the shops, buildings and other features depicted.

If you recognize anyone in the photographs in this book, or if you have information not already included in the author's caption, do let us know. We would love to hear from you, and will try to publish it in future books or articles.

Our production team

Frith books are produced by a small dedicated team at offices in the converted Grade II listed 18th-century barn at Teffont near Salisbury, illustrated above. Most have worked with the Frith Collection for many years. All have in common one quality: they have a passion for the Frith Collection. The team is constantly expanding, but currently includes:

Jason Buck, John Buck, Douglas Burns, Ruth Butler, Heather Crisp, Isobel Hall, Hazel Heaton, Peter Horne, James Kinnear, Tina Leary, Sue Molloy, Hannah Marsh, Kate Rotondetto, Dean Scource, Eliza Sackett, Terence Sackett, Sandra Sanger, Lewis Taylor, and Shelley Tolcher.